BUSINESS ISSUES, COMPETITION AND ENTREPRENEURSHIP

IMMIGRANT ENTREPRENEURSHIP IN THE U. S.

BUSINESS ISSUES, COMPETITION AND ENTREPRENEURSHIP

Additional books in this series can be found on Nova's website at:

https://www.novapublishers.com/catalog/index.php?cPath=23_29&seriesp=Business+Issues%2C+Competition+and+Entrepreneurship

Additional e-books in this series can be found on Nova's website at:

https://www.novapublishers.com/catalog/index.php?cPath=23_29&seriespe=Business+Issues%2C+Competition+and+Entrepreneurship

BUSINESS ISSUES, COMPETITION AND ENTREPRENEURSHIP

IMMIGRANT ENTREPRENEURSHIP IN THE U. S.

CHRISTIAN D. KNOWLES
EDITOR

Nova Science Publishers, Inc.
New York

Copyright © 2010 by Nova Science Publishers, Inc.

All rights reserved. No part of this book may be reproduced, stored in a retrieval system or transmitted in any form or by any means: electronic, electrostatic, magnetic, tape, mechanical photocopying, recording or otherwise without the written permission of the Publisher.

For permission to use material from this book please contact us:
Telephone 631-231-7269; Fax 631-231-8175
Web Site: http://www.novapublishers.com

NOTICE TO THE READER

The Publisher has taken reasonable care in the preparation of this book, but makes no expressed or implied warranty of any kind and assumes no responsibility for any errors or omissions. No liability is assumed for incidental or consequential damages in connection with or arising out of information contained in this book. The Publisher shall not be liable for any special, consequential, or exemplary damages resulting, in whole or in part, from the readers' use of, or reliance upon, this material. Any parts of this book based on government reports are so indicated and copyright is claimed for those parts to the extent applicable to compilations of such works.

Independent verification should be sought for any data, advice or recommendations contained in this book. In addition, no responsibility is assumed by the publisher for any injury and/or damage to persons or property arising from any methods, products, instructions, ideas or otherwise contained in this publication.

This publication is designed to provide accurate and authoritative information with regard to the subject matter covered herein. It is sold with the clear understanding that the Publisher is not engaged in rendering legal or any other professional services. If legal or any other expert assistance is required, the services of a competent person should be sought. FROM A DECLARATION OF PARTICIPANTS JOINTLY ADOPTED BY A COMMITTEE OF THE AMERICAN BAR ASSOCIATION AND A COMMITTEE OF PUBLISHERS.

Library of Congress Cataloging-in-Publication Data

Immigrant entrepreneurship in the U.S. / editor, Christian D. Knowles.
  p. cm.
  Includes index.
  ISBN 978-1-60876-816-5 (hardcover)
  1. Minority business enterprises--United States. 2. Entrepreneurship--United States. I. Knowles, Christian D.
  HD2358.5.U6147 2009
  338'.040869120973--dc22
                        2009046491

Published by Nova Science Publishers, Inc. † New York

CONTENTS

Preface		vii
Chapter 1	High-Tech Immigrant Entrepreneurship in the United States *David M. Hart, Zoltan J. Acs and Spencer L. Tracy*	1
Chapter 2	Estimating the Contribution of Immigrant Business Owners to the U.S. Economy *Robert W. Fairlie*	69
Index		109

PREFACE

A better understanding of how immigrants contribute to the U.S. economy is important. Few studies have examined how immigrant entrepreneurs contribute to total U.S. business ownership, formation, and income. This book examines the contributions of immigrant business owners and their businesses to the U.S. economy. The role of immigrants in high-tech entrepreneurship in the U.S. is also quantified. Among other findings, it was determined that nearly 1.5 million immigrant business owners in the U.S. represent 12.5 percent of all business owners. Moreover, the total business income generated by immigrant business owners is $67 billion, 11.6 percent of all business income in the U.S. In addition, although business owners from Mexico constitute the largest share of immigrant business owners, immigrants from around the world are sources of U.S. business formation, ownership and income. These findings indicate that immigrants make large and important contributions to business ownership, formation, and income in the U.S., particularly in some states and economic sectors. This book consists of public documents which have been located, gathered, combined, reformatted, and enhanced with a subject index, selectively edited and bound to provide easy access.

Chapter 1 - In this study, we quantify the role of immigrants in high-tech entrepreneurship in the United States. We report the results of a survey of a nationally representative sample of rapidly growing high-impact, high-tech companies.[1] This group of companies is very important to the U.S. economy, because they account for a disproportionate share of job creation and economic growth. We find that about 16% of the companies in our sample had at least one foreign-born person among their founding teams. This estimate is lower than that found in most previous studies of high-tech immigrant entrepreneurship.

Nonetheless, our data show that immigrants play a crucial role in this vital economic activity.

Chapter 2 - A better understanding of how immigrants contribute to the U.S. economy is important. Few studies have examined how immigrant entrepreneurs contribute to total U.S. business ownership, formation, and income. Using data from three large, nationally representative government datasets—the 2000 Census 5 percent Public Use Microdata (PUMS) Sample, the 1996-2007 Current Population Survey (CPS), and the 1992 Characteristics of Business Owners (CBO)—this study examines the contributions of immigrant business owners and their businesses to the U.S. economy.

Chapter 1

HIGH-TECH IMMIGRANT ENTREPRENEURSHIP IN THE UNITED STATES[*]

David M. Hart, Zoltan J. Acs and Spencer L. Tracy

EXECUTIVE SUMMARY

In this study, we quantify the role of immigrants in high-tech entrepreneurship in the United States. We report the results of a survey of a nationally representative sample of rapidly growing high-impact, high-tech companies.[1] This group of companies is very important to the U.S. economy, because they account for a disproportionate share of job creation and economic growth. We find that about 16% of the companies in our sample had at least one foreign-born person among their founding teams. This estimate is lower than that found in most previous studies of high-tech immigrant entrepreneurship. Nonetheless, our data show that immigrants play a crucial role in this vital economic activity.

High-impact, high-tech companies founded by immigrant entrepreneurs and those founded by native-born entrepreneurs in our sample are similar in many ways. They operate in the same industries and are about the same size.

---

[*] This is an edited, reformatted and augmented version of a Small Business Administration publication dated July 2009.

One important difference between the two is their location. Immigrant-founded companies tend to be located in states that have large immigrant populations. Another difference is that immigrant-founded companies in our sample are about twice as likely as native-founded companies to state that they have a strategic relationship with a foreign firm, such as a major supplier, key partner, or major customer. Immigrant-founded companies may also have a higher level of technological performance than native-founded companies, although the evidence on this issue is not conclusive.

This study sheds light on high-tech immigrant entrepreneurs as individuals as well as on the companies that they helped to found. The vast majority of these individuals are strongly rooted in the United States. A large proportion of them have lived in this country for two decades or more. More than three-quarters of them are U.S. citizens. Two-thirds of them received undergraduate or graduate degrees here. The 250 foreign-born entrepreneurs on whom we have data hail from 54 countries in all regions of the world. India is the largest source country, accounting for 16% of this group, followed by the U.K. at 10%.

Policymakers are rightly concerned that government should sustain a healthy climate for starting and running high-impact, high-tech companies like those in our sample. Immigration policy, as it affects highly educated and highly experienced foreign-born individuals who might be drawn into high-tech entrepreneurship, is an important element of that climate.

1.0. INTRODUCTION

A vigorous high-technology sector is vital to sustain U.S. prosperity in the 21st century. The new products, services, and business models that the high-tech sector generates differentiate this nation's output from that of the rest of the world and enable capital accumulation, wage gains, and productivity growth. A high level of entrepreneurship, by which we mean the founding of new businesses, makes the high-tech sector vigorous. High-tech entrepreneurs, by which we mean the founders of new high-tech businesses, take risks that managers of existing high-tech businesses choose not to take and recognize opportunities that they fail to spot.

High-tech entrepreneurship requires a rare combination of inclinations, capabilities, and resources. Half of new businesses fail within five years (Shane 2008), so founders must be optimistic, but also capable of weathering severe challenges. Because the opportunities in high-tech sectors blend together technological and market factors, individual entrepreneurs and founding teams in these sectors typically combine technical expertise rooted in formal education with market savvy that flows from extensive business experience. They must also be able to tap quickly and effectively into networks of customers, suppliers, expertise, finance, and talent as business opportunities ripen.

Foreign-born individuals play an important role in U.S. high-tech entrepreneurship. By virtue of having left their native land, they may have entrepreneurial inclinations. Their large presence in American higher education and the U.S. labor force, especially science and engineering disciplines and occupations, equips them with valuable knowledge that bears on high-tech innovation. Their outsider status may allow them, in some cases, to recognize "out-of-the box" opportunities that native-born individuals with similar knowledge and skills do not perceive. These capabilities may be linked to unique entrepreneurial resources, such as access to partners, customers, and suppliers in their countries of origin.

In this study, we quantify the role of immigrants[2] in high-tech entrepreneurship in a nationally representative sample of rapidly growing "high-impact" companies (HICs). This class of companies drives job creation and aggregate growth in the United States. We find that, while most previous studies have overstated the role of immigrants in high-tech entrepreneurship, it is nonetheless very important. For instance, about 16% of the companies in our sample had at least one foreign-born entrepreneur among their founding teams, and these high-tech companies display better performance in some respects than high-tech companies in our sample whose founders were all native-born. We also provide a profile of high-tech immigrant entrepreneurs. The vast majority are strongly rooted in the United States. Most of them received their highest educational degree here and have become citizens.

Our report begins by situating the subject of high-tech immigrant entrepreneurship in policy and analytical debates about immigration, entrepreneurship, and technology-based economic development. We then describe our methods and findings. We conclude by highlighting the research and policy agendas that our work illuminates.

2.0. POLICY CONTEXT

Our research brings together two important areas of public policy: technology-based economic development (TBED) and immigration. In both areas, recent research points to new ways to achieve desirable policy outcomes. The linkages between them are just beginning to be explored.

2.1. Technological Innovation, Entrepreneurship, and Economic Growth

The importance of technological innovation in economic growth is by now firmly established. Well-understood by classical economists, technology's contribution to the economy began to be conceptualized and measured after World War II by modern economists such as Solow (1957), Griliches (1958), Nelson (1959), and Arrow (1962). Applied economists in fields like industrial organization (Scherer 1984) and agricultural economics (Ruttan 2001) sustained this agenda, and they have been joined in recent years by formal theorists such as Romer (1990) and Lucas (1988). As McCraw (2007) has written, the twenty-first century is shaping up to be "Schumpeter's Century," a tribute to Joseph A. Schumpeter (1942), the towering figure whose work on technological innovation, entrepreneurship, and economic growth in the first half of the twentieth century set the stage for the advances of the post-World War II period.

Early studies of technology and economic growth in the post-World War II period centered on the contributions of formal R&D. Economic dynamism in these decades was perceived to flow from the investments made by large organizations with big R&D budgets, including public agencies, like the Department of Defense and the National Aeronautics and Space Administration, and multinational companies, such as IBM and General Electric. In his 1952 book *American Capitalism*, John Kenneth Galbraith described the large company as an "an almost perfect instrument" of technological development. Galbraith argued that oligopoly provided a sufficient level of competition to stimulate innovation, while also assuring an adequate resource flow to fund large-scale R&D operations and sufficient confidence that the benefits of these investments would be reaped by firms that built such operations.

This conventional wisdom was not entirely accurate. Beneath the giant redwoods of the Fortune 500, the industrial landscape of the United States contained a thriving undergrowth of smaller and newer companies in the 1950s and 1960s, including some seedlings that would grow into giants themselves, toppling their elders as they did so (Acs and Audretsch 1990). The post-World War II period heralded not only the expansion of large U.S.-based multinational companies but also the invention of whole new institutional forms, such as the venture capital firm and the high-tech start-up, which would eventually blossom into a unique entrepreneurial ecology in places like California's Silicon Valley and Boston's Route 128 (Kenney 2000, Hsu and Kenney 2005). Indeed, the environment in the United States for high-growth, high-tech start-up companies grew more hospitable over time, culminating in the entrepreneurial frenzy of the dot-com boom at the end of the twentieth century.

Recent research suggests that high-growth entrepreneurship is linked to a variety of important economic outcomes. Acs and Audretsch and their collaborators have shown in several studies that business start-ups are associated with economic growth at the regional and national levels. For instance, Acs and Mueller (2008) demonstrate that sustained economic benefits from entrepreneurship at the regional level derive mainly from young (two to five years old), medium-sized (20 to 499 employees) enterprises and not from small businesses in general or the establishment of branch plants of large firms. Haltiwanger (2009) provides evidence that companies that are less than five years old account for nearly all net job creation in the United States. Autio (2005) summarizes a variety of studies (including Wong, Ho, and Autio 2005) showing that 1-10% of new firms generate 40-75% of new jobs. Henrekson and Johansson (2008, 14) summarize the "clear-cut result" in empirical literature covering several countries, including the United States: "a few rapidly growing companies generate a disproportionately large share of all new net jobs..." In addition, as Scherer (1992) points out, competition from new entrants, even if they fail, forces their older rivals to adapt or die and thus drives productivity growth across the broader economy.

Although young, high-growth companies are present in a wide variety of industries, the dynamics of those in high-technology sectors are especially important for scholars and policymakers to understand. These companies are more likely than others to be pursuing opportunities associated with radical innovations that produce positive knowledge externalities and that may have transformative consequences for society (Baumol, Litan, and Schramm 2007). Because such opportunities are so challenging and so risky, existing businesses are particularly unlikely to find out about them or to pursue them (Utterback 1994, Christensen and Rosenbloom 1995). High-technology start-ups are one of the main organizational vehicles by which new knowledge in the science and engineering disciplines is converted into economic benefits (Acs, et al. 2005, Acs, Audretsch, and Strom 2009).

It is not surprising, then, that the federal government has made significant efforts to foster technological innovation, at first mainly by investing in R&D and more recently by seeking to stimulate entrepreneurship, especially in high-tech sectors. The federal R&D budget is about $150 billion per year, to which more than $20 billion was added for FY09 and FY10 by the American Recovery and Reinvestment Act of February 2009. Since 1982, a designated fraction of this budget across the major R&D agencies has been devoted to the Small Business Innovation Research (SBIR) program, which supports many innovative small companies (Wessner 2007). The SBIR set-aside has risen from 0.2% of each agency's external research budget at the program's outset to 2.5% in recent years. The creation of SBIR program in 1982 was part of a larger package of federal policy initiatives that began in the late 1970s and helped channel support to high-tech start-ups. These initiatives included the relaxation of the "prudent man" rule for venture capital investment (which allowed pension funds to invest a small fraction of their portfolios in venture firms) in 1978, the 1980 Bayh-Dole Act governing intellectual property generated by federal R&D funding, the National Cooperative Research Act of 1984, and the reorientation and renaming of the National Institute of Standards and Technology in 1988 (Hart 1998, Hughes 2005, Graham 1992).

Many state governments reached the conclusion that technology-based economic development (TBED) deserved their attention in the same period or even earlier. North Carolina's development of Research Triangle Park is a pioneering example that dates back to the 1950s. In addition to seeking to capitalize on federal R&D funding, including SBIR, states have experimented with a wide variety of programs, including support for academic R&D and technology transfer, venture capital investment, loan programs for small businesses, workforce upgrading, and more (Clarke and Gaile 1989, Waits 2000, Pages, Friedman, and von Bargen 2003). The central goal of these diverse efforts was to enable organic growth of existing businesses within the state and to nurture new businesses, rather than to chase the elusive "smokestacks" (that is, branch plants of large enterprises) that might move to the state from elsewhere.[3] Peter Eisinger (1988) captured the trend for scholars in his book *The Rise of the Entrepreneurial State*, and David Osborne (1988) popularized it the same year in *Laboratories of Democracy*. A recent review of state initiatives in economic development by the National Governors Association (NGA) shows that TBED policy momentum at the state level has been sustained, as states seek to shift the basis of competitive advantage from cost reduction to knowledge creation, innovation, and entrepreneurship (NGA 2006).

The contribution of immigration to entrepreneurially oriented TBED has not gone unnoticed. American universities, for example, have long argued that their ability to attract the best students and faculty regardless of nationality was an essential element of the country's global leadership in science and, by extension, high-tech innovation. Recent developments have drawn greater attention on this issue. From Richard Florida's (2003) use of a "melting-pot index" to explain high-tech entrepreneurship at the regional level to the debate over the H-1B visa program, which is described in the next section, U.S. policymakers are focused as never before on the linkage between foreign-born talent and high-tech entrepreneurship.

2.2. Immigration

The U.S. immigration system is quite complex. Navigating it can be difficult both for applicants, who seek to come to the United States or to change their immigration status while in this country, and for their sponsors, such as family members and employers. The system is administered by the U.S. Department of Homeland Security (DHS) and U.S. Citizenship and Immigration Services (USCIS) within DHS. The status of legal permanent residence (also known as the "green card") permits the holder most of the same rights as U.S. citizens. Legal permanent residents may also choose to naturalize and become citizens. Nonimmigrant visas permit temporary residence in the United States. There are many types of nonimmigrant visas, and they authorize their holders to undertake some activities, while restricting others. For instance, student visa holders may not be allowed to work as much as they might like, while the holders of certain temporary employment visas, such as the H-1B, may be unable to change employers. Nonimmigrant visa holders may be able to adjust their status to legal permanent residence if they meet certain eligibility requirements. For instance, a nonimmigrant visa holder may become eligible for status adjustment through marriage to a U.S. citizen or because their employer sponsors them. Half or more of all lawful immigration to the United States in most years is accounted for by status adjustment.

The economic implications of immigration are of great public importance. Public interest has concentrated especially on the economic impact of the unskilled and poorly educated workers who constitute the bulk of the immigrant flow. Some advocates argue that these immigrants fill necessary jobs that would otherwise go wanting, especially so-called "3D" (dirty, difficult, and dangerous) jobs (Koser 2007). Others argue that low-skill immigration displaces native-born workers and drives down wages. Both positions find some support in the scholarly literature. Borjas (1999), for one, argues that low-skill immigration redistributes wealth from low-skill natives to high-skill natives and the owners of capital. Card (2005, 2) counters that "evidence that immigrants have harmed the opportunities of less educated natives is scant," while Ottaviano and Peri (2006) find that once the economy equilibrates most native workers actually benefit from immigration.

High-skill immigration cannot be entirely separated from this broad debate about the economic impact of immigration. The annual quota for legal permanent residence, for instance, must be divided among immigrants at all skill levels, which means that policymakers must weigh the merits of high-skill immigration against those of low-skill immigration. The distribution of approximately one million green cards each year is currently dominated by low-skill applicants. Applicants who have family ties to the United States, who are predominantly low-skill, receive about two-thirds of these places, while only about 11% are awarded to principal applicants on the basis of their job skills. Proposals to expand the share of employment-based green cards and to institute a "point system" that would have benefited the highly skilled met with fierce resistance from defenders of the current system during the 2007 immigration debate in Congress.

In addition to being linked legislatively and administratively, the debates about high-skill and low-skill immigration are linked ideologically and analytically. Advocates of a more expansive immigration policy claim that highly skilled immigrants fill positions that natives will not or cannot fill. These are not "3D" jobs, as in low-skill immigration, but rather highly technical ones in the science, technology, engineering, and mathematics (STEM) fields. American students, responding to the national culture and the educational system, they argue, have lost the taste for entering such challenging fields. Andrescu et al. (2008, 1256), for instance, argue that "it is deemed uncool within the social context of USA middle and high schools to do mathematics for fun; doing so can lead to social ostracism." Yet, educating

STEM students and filling STEM jobs (often with students and recent graduates from other countries), the argument continues, is essential to drive technology-based economic growth. House Speaker Nancy Pelosi, echoing the National Academy of Sciences report *Rising Above the Gathering Storm* (2005), recently called for the country to be more aggressive in recruiting highly skilled immigrants, for instance, by "stapling a green card to the diploma" of foreign graduate students (Mervis 2009). These advocates find support in studies like those of Kerr and Lincoln (2008) and Hunt and Gauthier-Loiselle (2008), which use patent data to demonstrate a "crowding-in" effect, in which the presence of foreign-born inventors stimulates more native-born invention.

Advocates of a more restrictive policy argue that highly skilled immigrants "crowd-out" their native-born counterparts. The Economic Policy Institute (2007), for example, argues that some measures under debate, such as the expansion of the H-1B visa program, which is described below, would lead to more offshore outsourcing (that is, the use of contractors based outside the United States), lower wages, and reduced job opportunities for technology industry workers. The share of native-born students interested in STEM fields up through the undergraduate level, this perspective maintains, has not declined. However, many of these students leave these fields in response to labor market signals that reveal that their earnings will be substantially higher in other fields, such as law and finance (Lowell and Salzman 2007). Advocates on this side of the debate can cite in support of their views the work of scholars like Borjas (2005), who estimates that a 10% rise in foreign doctoral students in a field depresses wages by about 3%, and Levin et al. (2004), who find that foreign doctoral recipients displace the native-born from science and engineering positions.

The H-1B visa, a category of nonimmigrant visa for highly skilled workers, illustrates the situation well. This visa was created by the Immigration Act of 1990, which significantly expanded immigration overall, with a cap of 65,000 per year. The cap was tripled by Congress in the late 1 990s, as high-tech companies clamored for qualified help during the Internet boom. It has since returned to its original level, but because H-1B visa holders can stay in the country for up to six years and because of a variety of exemptions to the cap, an estimated 500,000 or more now reside here (Lowell 2006). Both sides of the debate find support in the H-1B experience. Kierkegaard (2007, 72), for instance, concludes that H-1B visa holders are "complements to U.S. workers, rather than substitutes." Lowell (quoted in

Bhattacharjee 2007), on the other hand, views the H-1B as "de facto bondage" to employers, which depresses salaries of native workers.

After the failure of the 2007 immigration bill in Congress, the U.S. immigration policy debate receded somewhat,[4] but the global context in which it is being made remains quite dynamic, especially with regard to high-skill migration (Skills Research Initaitive 2008). Traditional countries of immigration that have long favored the highly skilled, such as Canada and Australia, continue to adjust their policies to maintain or expand the flow of these immigrants. Canada, for instance, now attracts about ten times as many educated immigrants relative to its population as the United States does, although unlike the United States, it also loses many highly educated workers through emigration (mainly to the United States) (National Science Board 2008). The high-skill immigration policies of the smaller English-speaking countries have a "Red Queen" aspect to them – they have to run harder just to stay in the same place, as Lewis Carroll's character famously described herself in *Through the Looking Glass*.

Countries that have not historically been receptive to immigration, like Germany and Japan, have also stepped up their efforts to attract scientific and technical talent (Hart 2006). The European Union as a whole is in the midst of launching a "Blue Card" program that aims to attract highly skilled migrants to Europe and facilitate their movement within the EU (EurActiv 2008). Middle- and lower-income countries are now in the global talent game as well. The successful strategies of Taiwan, Ireland, and Israel, which entered high-tech sectors while wooing home expatriates from Silicon Valley, are being emulated by China and India, among others (Saxenian 2006). Countries of emigration like these are also making more aggressive efforts to retain talented young people who in the past would have seen going abroad as their only viable option for professional success and entrepreneurial opportunity.

It would be inaccurate to conclude that the United States has lost its place as the central hub of the global system for high-skill migration. The foreign student population in the United States is growing and recently hit an all-time high, new restrictions imposed after 9/11 and new competition abroad notwithstanding (Lowell et al. 2007, Institute of International Education 2008). The H-1B visa cap of 65,000 was over-subscribed on the first day that applications were permitted in 2008 and will likely be hit again in 2009.[5] The backlog for employment-based green cards totals more than 500,000 applicants (Wadhwa et al 2007a). These figures indicate that demand for entrance into the United States remains strong. Policymakers face difficult choices about how to respond to this demand and to improve current policy.

3.0. THEORETICAL CONTEXT

Our research answers the empirical question "how many high-tech immigrant entrepreneurs are there?" In this section, we describe why this question is interesting from a theoretical perspective. There are, in fact, theoretical reasons to think both that the foreign-born will be *over*-represented in high-tech entrepreneurship and that they will be *under*-represented. Building on the seminal work of Shane and Venkataraman (2000), we define entrepreneurship as the creation, recognition, and exploitation of opportunities to supply future goods and services. The creation of opportunities is a societal function, but the characteristics of individual entrepreneurs, including their nativity, influences whether they recognize and exploit these opportunities (Hart forthcoming).

3.1. Recognition of Entrepreneurial Opportunity

Scholarly understanding of how and why entrepreneurs recognize opportunities is incomplete. Some part of the process may never be entirely comprehensible from the outside, depending on an ineffable "flash of creative genius," (as Justice William O. Douglas famously described the process of invention in *Cuno Engineering* (1941)), on timing, and on luck. But we can say with some confidence that recognition of entrepreneurial opportunity depends in part on psychological attributes and in part on knowledge and experience, with the latter weighing particularly heavily in high-tech entrepreneurship. And we know that foreign-born residents of the United States are different in both of these respects from the native-born.

The most commonly accepted distillation of the psychological element of entrepreneurial opportunity recognition is "alertness" (Kirzner 1973). Some people are on the lookout for opportunities, while others are not. This attribute seems to be passed down through families; the children of entrepreneurs are more likely than others to become entrepreneurs themselves (Lentz and Laband 1990). Immigrants may also be more "alert" in this sense than the average native-born person. Those who come to the United States for education or employment, for instance, have, at a minimum, recognized opportunities for personal achievement outside the borders of their native land. This group is the end product of a self-selection process that separates them from those in their home countries who do not migrate, in part on the basis of the capacity to recognize opportunities (Borjas 1990).

Educational attainment is easier to measure than "alertness." High-tech entrepreneurs have higher levels of educational attainment than the general public. The Global Entrepreneurship Monitor finds, for instance, that nascent entrepreneurs who expect to create many jobs are better educated than other entrepreneurs (Bullvaag 2006). High-tech entrepreneurs are also more likely to have degrees in science and engineering (S&E) disciplines than other fields. The foreign-born are disproportionately represented in these disciplines in U.S. higher education. Foreign students constituted 25% of all S&E graduate students in 2005, with the highest concentrations in engineering (45%) and computer sciences (43%) (NSB 2008, p. 2-21). The National Science Board points out that "[n]oncitizens, primarily those with temporary visas, account for the bulk of the growth in S&E doctorates awarded by U.S. universities from 1985 through 2005... The temporary resident share of S&E doctorates rose from 21% in 1985 to 36% in 2005" (NSB 2008, pp. 2-31).

Many foreign students, perhaps two-thirds of them, stay in the United States after graduation and join the labor force. Given their academic training, it is not surprising that the foreign- born are disproportionately present in S&E occupations. The U.S. Census Bureau, for instance, estimates that 26% of college-educated workers in such occupations were foreign born, compared to their 12% share of the overall population (NSB 2008). (See also Table 15 below). This population has been growing steadily in recent years. "In the 2000 census, about 43% of all college-educated, foreign-born individuals in S&E occupations (62% of doctorate holders) reported arriving in the United States after 1990" (NSB 2008, pp. 3-50). The formal knowledge reaped from their education and the business experience gained from their work combine to provide the prerequisites for over-representation of the foreign-born in U.S. high- tech entrepreneurship.

Although their educational and occupational backgrounds are similar, foreign-born high-tech entrepreneurs may recognize different opportunities than their native-born counterparts. As Carlsson and Jacobson (1997) put it (in a different context), the blending of cultures experienced by immigrants may enlarge the "search space" in which opportunities are sought. Immigrants may see, for instance, potential markets or supply chain relationships in their native lands that are not visible to those who lack their knowledge, language ability, and experience. People holding diverse values may also resolve uncertainties about the same opportunity differently. These differences may then drive disagreements about how promising that opportunity is, leading to spin-offs from existing businesses, and start-ups of brand new companies, to exploit that opportunity. The work of Florida (2003, 2005) and Ottaviano and Peri (2006) suggest that there is an association between social diversity due to foreign and domestic nativity on the one hand and levels of entrepreneurship at the regional and national levels on the other.

We have emphasized in this section the theoretical factors that lead us to hypothesize that the foreign-born will be over-represented in high-tech entrepreneurship, but we also want to point out as well that there are factors that pull in the opposite direction. Language barriers, for instance, may make it difficult for even highly educated and well-experienced foreign-born technical experts to recognize entrepreneurial opportunities quickly enough to seize them. Indeed, language barriers may channel immigrants into fields in which their language skills are less important. Language proficiency in general is the most important determinant of immigrant success in the labor market (Borjas 1999). Foreign-born experts may also be more likely to pursue (or to be shunted into) technical career ladders and get off of the management track. This career path leads to less exposure to market trends and customer feedback that may give rise to the "flash of creative genius" that sparks an entrepreneurial venture.

3.2. Exploitation of Entrepreneurial Opportunity

It is one thing to recognize an entrepreneurial opportunity and another to take advantage of it by creating a new business. Like recognition of opportunity, exploitation of opportunity involves both the attitudes and the attributes of the entrepreneur. The foreign-born and native-born populations differ in important ways with respect to both. These differences, more so than those that bear on opportunity recognition, provide arguments both for and against over-representation of the foreign-born among U.S. high-tech entrepreneurs.

We can conceive of the attitudinal factors that determine entrepreneurial behavior as involving both rational calculation and speculative risk-taking. Rational calculation involves the financial tradeoff of giving up, at least temporarily, what is usually a reasonably secure and remunerative position for a new and uncertain career trajectory. This calculus may also encompass the utility derived from personal satisfaction and social esteem that flow from one's choice. The foreign-born may have less to lose from taking the entrepreneurial plunge than the native-born in these respects, particularly if discrimination blocks their promotion within existing businesses (Bates and Dunham 1993). The opportunity cost of entrepreneurship is lower in such a circumstance. On the other hand, they may also perceive greater difficulties in getting back on their old career track in the likely case of failure, and so be reluctant to become entrepreneurs.

The rational calculation of costs and benefits is inevitably incomplete, and potential entrepreneurs must fill in the gaps with guesses and beliefs. For those who move forward in entrepreneurship, these guesses and beliefs typically reflect optimism and a penchant for risk. The stereotypical immigrant in American folklore possesses just these qualities, suggesting that foreign-born individuals will more likely make the decision to start a company than native-born individuals with similar backgrounds. However, this stereotype does not characterize all highly skilled immigrants. For some, the reasons for immigration may have less to do with seeking a fortune than with finding secure and well-compensated employment, in which case their decisions will be biased against entrepreneurship.

The exploitation of high-tech opportunities requires that entrepreneurs draw not only on their own resources, but also on those of colleagues and of society more broadly. These resources include money, talent, contacts, and knowledge. Access to these resources quickly and at a reasonable cost depends on the entrepreneurs' social capital – that is, the networks in which they are embedded and the levels of trust that exist in these networks – and the social institutions that surround the high-tech start-up process. Some key networks in the U.S. high-tech sector, most notably those that provide access to venture capital, seem to be composed of "bonding" social capital, created through ties of age, gender, and ethnicity. Brush (2003), for example, shows that female entrepreneurs tend to be excluded from these networks, and the foreign-born may suffer from a similar process of discrimination in seeking financial support.

The dominance of traditional forms of "bonding" social capital ought to reduce the probability that foreign-born entrepreneurs can effectively exploit the opportunities that they perceive. Saxenian (2006), though, has shown that, at least in some cases, foreign-born high-tech entrepreneurs take effective advantage of their own "bonding" social capital in the form of networks of co-ethnics and linkages to their countries of origin. Ethnic professional associations and alumni clubs, for instance, provide access to potential new hires and funders. The Indus Entrepreneurs, an organization of U.S. residents from South Asia, for example, aims to enhance the social capital of its membership. Some foreign governments have also enacted "diaspora policies" that support these kinds of networks and even provide venture capital to high-tech entrepreneurs abroad. Scotland, Chile, South Africa, and Armenia are among the countries that have undertaken such policies, demonstrating the breadth of the appeal of this idea (Ionescu 2006, Kuznetsov and Sabel 2006).

We can conclude that theory does not provide conclusive guidance about the relative representation of foreign-born and native-born in the population of high-tech entrepreneurs. Although like most others in this field, we would expect the factors that predict overrepresentation to dominate those that predict under-representation, the issue can best be resolved through empirical observation of the sort that we have undertaken.

4.0. PRIOR RESEARCH

Empirical research on immigrant entrepreneurship in the United States is growing. In recent years, several authors have examined high-tech entrepreneurship. However, no study before this one has focused on the role of immigrant entrepreneurs in the key companies that drive job creation and growth in the U.S. economy.

4.1. Immigrant Entrepreneurship in General

Research on immigrant entrepreneurship is dominated by the study of self-employment, ethnic enclaves, and, most recently, "transnationalism."[6] This literature finds that the foreign-born are more likely to start companies than the native-born (Fairlie 2008, Light and Rosenstein 1995). The self-employment rate for foreign-born residents of the United States has grown much faster than that of native-born residents over the past ten years (U.S. Small Business Administration 2007). Most of these businesses, like most of those started by the native-born, remain very small, often employing no one other than the owner. Immigrant- founded companies play key roles in creating and sustaining ethnic communities in major U.S. cities, such as New York, Los Angeles, and Miami (Light and Gold 2000). Business networks, populated by highly educated managers and entrepreneurs who have deep roots in the United States, link these communities to their countries of origin (Portes, Guarnizo, and Haller 2002). Immigrant entrepreneurs from particular ethnic groups tend to concentrate in specific niches, including high-skill as well as low-skill sectors (Fairlie 2008, Federman, Harrington, and Krynski 2006).

4.2. High-Tech Immigrant Entrepreneurship

Saxenian (1999) pioneered research focused specifically on high-tech immigrant entrepreneurship. She observed that Indians and Chinese were an increasingly visible presence within Silicon Valley and that many had founded start-ups there, in part because of the "glass ceiling" that blocked their promotion within existing high-tech companies. She discovered that 24% of Silicon Valley start-ups between 1980 and 1998 had CEOs with Chinese or Indian surnames, although she was unable to distinguish their location of birth. Qualitative research revealed that the Indian and Chinese high-tech communities, like ethnic enclaves in the rest of the economy, were sustained by a rich network of associations and maintained linkages to their countries of origin.

Saxenian's work demonstrates that high-tech immigrant entrepreneurship is very important for Silicon Valley (and for the home countries of the immigrants as well), but because it concentrates on the region of the United States in which high-tech immigrant entrepreneurs are most likely to be found, one cannot generalize easily from it. More recent studies by the National Venture Capital Association (Anderson and Platzer 2006) and the Massachusetts Biotechnology Association (Monti et al. 2007) have a similar positive selection bias in their approach to the subject and report similar results, a rate of immigrant founding of about 25%. Hsu et al. (2007) and Bhide (2008) also study elite groups, MIT alumni and venture capital-backed companies respectively, and find that non-U.S. citizens and foreign-born in these groups are more likely to be entrepreneurs than U.S. citizens and native-born.

Wadhwa et al. (2007b) seek to generalize Saxenian (1999) to the national level and update it with more recent data. They find that 25% of high-tech companies founded between 1995 and 2005 that had achieved more than $1 million in sales or employed more than 20 people had CEOs or chief technical officers (CTOs) who were born abroad. This is a valuable study, but it has important weaknesses. The $1 million size threshold excludes a large proportion of high-tech companies that may still be growing rapidly and making important economic contributions. By limiting "founder" to CEO or

CTO, the study may exclude up to half of all founders (Burton 1995, Hannan, Burton, and Baron 1996).

Table 1. Foreign-Born Share of High-Tech Entrepreneurship in the United States: Comparison of Studies

Author	Year Released	Population/Source	Estimated Share Foreign-Born	Definition
Hart et al. (this study)	2009	*Population:* High-impact companies in select SICs as identified in Acs et al. 2007 *Source:* CRB American Corporate Statistical Library	16%	Companies with at least one foreign-born founder (self-defined) as stated by survey respondent.
DesRoches et al.	2007	*Population:* Firms in select SICs founded in 2004 *Source:* Kauffman Firm Survey	16%	Companies with at least one foreignborn founder (self-defined) as stated by survey respondent.
Reynolds and Curtin	2007	*Population:* U.S. adults *Source:* Panel Study of Entrepreneurial Dynamics I and II	15%	Nascent entrepreneurs who expect to have substantial impact (50+ jobs) who reported being foreign-born.
Wadhwa et al.	2007	*Population:* Firms in select SICs with $1 MM+ sales, 20+ employees, 1995-2005 *Source:* D&B Million Dollar Database	25%	Companies with foreign-born CEO or CTO, as stated by respondent.
Monti, Smith-Doerr, and MacQuaid	2007	*Population:* Biotech firms founded in New England *Source:* Mass. Biotech. Assn. members list	26%	Companies with at least one foreign-born founder (self-defined) as stated by respondent or listed on company website.
Anderson and Platzer	2006	*Population:* Publicly traded, venture-backed companies that are still independent, 1990-2005 *Source:* Thomson Financial	25%	Companies with at least one foreign-born founder (self-defined), as stated by respondent or listed in public or Internet documents.
Saxenian	1999	*Population:* High-tech firms in select SICs founded in Silicon Valley, 1980-1998 *Source:* D&B custom database	24%	Companies that have CEOs with Chinese or Indian surnames.

Two large national survey projects yield results on the proportion of immigrant company founders that are substantially lower than those of Wadhwa et al. (2007b). The Kauffman Firm Survey (DesRoches et al. 2007), is a random sample of all companies founded in 2004, and it over-samples high-tech sectors.[7] About 16% of the companies in the high-tech sectors reported having at least one foreign-born founder. The weakness of this study for our purposes is that the sampling frame includes companies with zero or one employee, which constitute the vast majority of U.S. start-ups, but which do not account for very much net job creation or aggregate economic growth. The Panel Study of Entrepreneurial Dynamics is a representative national sample of individuals involved in business founding (Reynolds and Curtin 2007). Of those in this group who expected their companies to create 50 or more jobs after 5 years (about 5% of the sample), 15% were foreign-born. These results, too, are indicative, but not definitive, since they are based on expectations rather than outcomes and the absolute numbers involved are very small.

The main findings of the earlier studies covered in this section are summarized along with our own key findings in Table 1..

5.0. DATA AND METHODS

Our study focuses on foreign-born founders of "high-impact" companies (HICs) in high-tech sectors. As Acs, Parsons, and Tracy (2008) show, high-impact companies account for the bulk of job creation and economic growth in the United States. High-tech companies within this group are disproportionately important, because of the positive externalities they generate for companies in the rest of the economy. We conducted a professional-quality survey that produced a representative national random sample of these companies.

5.1. The American Corporate Statistical Library (A CSL)

The universe of companies from which our population and survey sample were drawn is the Corporate Research Board's American Corporate Statistical Library (ACSL). The ACSL is among the most comprehensive business databases in the United States, containing more than 140 variables on all firms in the country. The ACSL links each firm over time from its birth through any physical location moves it makes, capturing changes in ownership along the way, and recording the firm's death if it occurs. The result is a unique longitudinal business file that allows for analysis of the U.S. economy at the firm level. The Corporate Research Board updates the ACSL every 6 months, drawing on hundreds of public and private sector data sources.

5.2. 2007 SBA High-Impact Company Study

We draw upon prior SBA-sponsored work by Acs, Parsons, and Tracy (2008), which identified all HICs in the ACSL for the period 2002-2006. An HIC is a firm the sales of which have at least doubled over the most recent 4-year period and which has an employment growth quantifier of 2 or greater over the same period.[8] There were 376,605 HICs (approximately 2.2% of all companies) in the United States between 2002 and 2006.

5.3. Definition of Survey Population

From this group of HICs, we selected those classified by the ACSL as having their primary activity in a high-tech industry. An industry is defined as a 3-digit Standard Industrial Classification (SIC).[9] Our list of high-tech SICs appears in Appendix 1. There are 49 such industries, 44 in the manufacturing domain and five in the services domain. Our definition of "high-tech" draws heavily on the work of the Bureau of Labor Statistics (Hadlock, Hecker, and Gannon 1991), which uses R&D employment as a share of total employment as the key criterion. We also include several other industries that have a high ratio of R&D spending to total revenues, which are identified in Varga (1998). Our list of high-tech sectors is very similar to that used by the Kauffman Firm Survey. The total population of HICs for 2002- 2006 in our 49 high-tech SICs was about 24,000. Of these companies, 17,000 (about 70%) were in the five service SICs; the remaining 7,000 were in manufacturing sectors. Computer and data processing services (SIC 737) and engineering and architectural services (SIC 871) were the industries containing the largest number of HICs, together accounting for about half the total.[10]

5.4. Survey Method

Our strategy for the design of the survey questionnaire was to keep it short and focused. This approach boosts the response rate and minimizes respondent error. The questionnaire is attached as Appendix 2. It asks about the respondent company's technological and business activities in general terms, such as whether it has an R&D laboratory or holds patents. It then concentrates on the company's founders, gathering information for each founder about his or her home country, citizenship, length of residence in the United States, educational background, gender, race,[11] and relationship with other members of the founding team.

The survey was administered by the George Mason University Center for Social Science Research between October 2008 and January 2009. Telephone interviewers received general training as well as training specific to the questionnaire. For quality assurance purposes, supervisors used wireless headsets to monitor telephone interviews, providing both audio and visual access to interviewer performance. Telephone numbers were called up to eleven times at varying times of day, particularly during weekdays, with times varying to accommodate different time zones. To help maximize response rates, the computer-assisted telephone interviewing (CATI) system was programmed to make callbacks until a final disposition was reached. Interviewers set specific callback appointment times whenever appropriate, and these were automatically processed by the CATI program to be called at the specified time.

Of the nearly 24,000 HICs, we surveyed 2,668. This number was driven by two principal considerations: project resources and expected response rate. Of the 2,668 HICs surveyed, 1,415 provided completed responses, giving us a response rate of 53%. The number of responses to each question on the survey that are usable in our analysis varies from about 1,200 to about 1,350, because of respondent choice or interviewer error. These data were validated to ensure that they were representative of the full population of companies and were used to create two databases, one in which the unit of observation is the company and another in which the unit of observation is the founder. (Many companies have more than one founder, as described in more detail below.)

5.5. Analytic Methods

We use three basic methods for the analysis of the survey data, which are highlighted in the tables in this report. In some cases, we carry out cross-tabulations of two variables in order to see whether they are associated with one another in a non-random way. We use Pearson's chi-square test to assess the strength of the association. The results of this test are reported as a probability value (denoted as "P"), which describes the odds of the association being merely a matter of chance. If the probability value is .05, for instance, there is only a 1 in 20 chance that the two variables are associated with one another by chance, which is the level commonly used to define statistical significance.

The other two methods are regression methods, which seek to find associations between multiple variables. If the dependent variable takes on continuous values, such as company employment, we use linear regression. If the dependent variable is binary, such as an answer to a yes or no survey question, we use logistic regression. The purpose of these regressions is to explore whether an association between two variables found in a cross-tabulation remains strong when other variables that we also expect to have a relationship to the dependent variable are added to the analysis. These other variables are known as control variables. For instance, firm employment is likely to be related to company age, since we expect older companies to be bigger than younger companies. We therefore controlled for company age in our regression analyses that explored whether firms founded only by natives are larger than those in which at least one immigrant was a member of the founding team. Regression analysis yields a probability value that is similar to that produced by the Pearson's chi-square test for cross-tabulations described above. The smaller the P-value, the more likely it is that the association between the two variables is not a matter of chance. In the regression analyses, we weighted our sample data, so that they more closely resemble the full population of firms with respect to four variables: company age, company employment, manufacturing or service sector, and share of foreign-born population by state. Weighting allows us to be more confident that we can generalize from the analyses.

6.0. FINDINGS

The main findings of the survey are presented in this section. Our key finding is that about 16% of the companies in the sample reported that at least one of their founders was foreign-born (Tables 1 and 2). This rate is very close to the rate found by the Kauffman Firm Survey, despite the fact that the populations sampled were quite different. Eighty-one percent of the companies in our sample reported that all of their founders were born in the United States, and 3% of the respondents did not know the answer to this question or refused to answer it. Although the 16% rate is at the low end of the range of published studies reported above, it nonetheless represents a substantial fraction of HICs. The responses to other questions about the companies in our sample are provided in Table 2. These are analyzed in more detail in the following section.

6.1. Profile of Immigrant Founded Firms (IFCs)

The demographics of immigrant-founded companies (IFCs), those that have at least one foreign-born founder, are very similar to those of native-founded companies (NFCs), with the exception of their location. The distributions of the two groups of companies between manufacturing and services (Table 3) and across age categories (Table 4) were not significantly different in a chi-square test.

The distributions across SICs showed some statistically significant differences (for instance, IFCs are over-represented in business services and electronics), but the overall pattern is very similar to that of NFCs (Figure 1).

The locations of IFCs correspond with the locations of foreign-born populations generally. They are disproportionately concentrated in states with high and very high shares of foreign-born residents, such as California and Texas (Figure 2).

Table 2. High-Impact, High-Tech Company Survey: Descriptive Data

Question	Response Options/Number of Responses and Percent of Total					
Location (Share of Foreign-Born by State)	0-6% 497 (37.1%)	6.1-10% 210 (15.7%)	10.1+% 634 (47.3%)	Total Respondents 1,341		
Sector	Manufacturing 434 (32.4%)	Services 907 (67.6%)	Total Respondents 1,341			
Age (years)	<10 400 (31.1%)	10 to <20 532 (41.4%)	20 to <30 204 (15.9%)	30+ 149 (11.6%)	Total Respondents 1,285	
Publicly or Privately Held Company	Public 51 (3.8%)	Private 1,247 (93.9%)	Other/Don't Know/Refused 30 (2.2%)	Total Respondents 1,298		
Own R&D Lab	Yes 370 (27.6%)	No 959 (71.6%)	Don't Know or Refused 11 (.8%)	Total Respondents 1,340		
	Yes	No	Don't Know or Refused	Total Respondents		

Table 2. (Continued)

Question	Response Options/Number of Responses and Percent of Total					
Outside R&D Contracts	220 (16.9%)	1,047 (80.2%)	38 (2.9%)	1,305		
	Yes	No	Don't Know or Refused	Total Respondents		
Hold Patents	289 (21.6%)	983 (73.4%)	68 (5.1%)	1,340		
	Yes	No	Don't Know or Refused	Total Respondents		
Strategic Relationship with Foreign Firm	347 (25.9%)	958 (71.4%)	36 (2.7%)	1,341		
	1	2	3	4	5 or more	Total Respondents
Number of Founders	727 (54.9%)	433 (32.7%)	104 (7.8%)	35 (2.6%)	25 (1.9%)	1,324
	Family	Attended School or College Together	Worked Together Previously	Got Together to Start Business	Other or More Than 1 Reason	Don't Know or Refused
How Founders Brought Together	196 (28.1%)	52 (7.4%)	235 (33.7%)	95 (13.6%)	78 (11.2%)	42 (6.0%)
	No	Yes	Don't Know or Refused	Total Respondents		
At Least One Foreign-Born Founder	1,057 (80.7%)	205 (15.7%)	47 (3.6%)	1,309		

Source: Corporate Research Board, *High-Impact, High-Tech Company Survey Database* (2009).

In bivariate tests of economic performance, IFCs outperform NFCs. We use company employment to measure economic performance, because it is generally regarded as more reliable in the D&B data than company revenue. Using three categories of company employment (1-4 employees, 5-20 employees, and 21 or more employees), we found that IFCs are more likely to be in the larger two categories to a statistically significant degree. In particular, about 33% of the IFCs were in the largest employment group, compared with about 24% of the NFCs (Table 5). However regression results generally suggest that controlling for other factors, such as company age and the founders' educational level, washes out this result. In most specifications, when these control variables are added to the analysis, the coefficient on the nativity of the founder is no longer significantly different from zero (Table 6).
Note: Number of responses may vary by question.

Table 3. High-Impact, High-Tech Companies by Founder Nativity and Economic Sector

Sector	Native-Founded	Immigrant-Founded	TOTAL
Manufacturing	343 (32.6%)	56 (27.3%)	399 (31.7%)
Service	709 (67.4%)	149 (72.7%)	858 (68.3%)
TOTAL	1,052 (100%)	205 (100%)	1257 (100%)

Source: Corporate Research Board, *High-Impact, High-Tech Company Survey Database* (2009). Note: Pearson chi-squared (1) = 2.21. P = 0.14.

Table 4. High-Impact, High-Tech Companies by Founder Nativity and Company Age

Age	Native-Founded	Immigrant-Founded	TOTAL
Less than 10 years	305 (30.2%)	69 (34.3%)	374 (30.9%)
10 to less than 20 years	415 (41.0%)	83 (41.3%)	498 (41.1%)
20 to less than 30 years	171 (16.9%)	27 (13.4%)	198 (16.3%)
30 years and above	120 (11.9%)	22 (10.9%)	142 (11.7%)
TOTAL	1,011 (100%)	201 (100%)	1,212 (100%)

Source: Corporate Research Board, *High-Impact, High-Tech Company Survey Database* (2009). Note: Pearson chi-squared (3) = 2.31. P = 0.51.

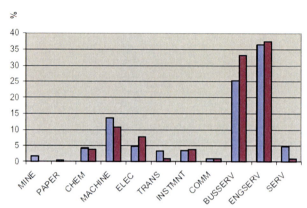

Source: Corporate Research Board, *High-Impact, High-Tech Company Survey Database* (2009).

Note: Mine = Mining, Chem = Chemicals, Machine = Machinery, Elec = Electronics, Trans = Transportation Equipment, Instmnt = Instruments, Comm = Communications Equipment, Busserv = Business Services, Engserv = Engineering Services, Serv = Other Services.

Figure 1. High-Impact, High-Tech Companies by Founder Nativity and 2-Digit SIC.

Source: Corporate Research Board, *High-Impact, High-Tech Company Survey Database* (2009).

Figure 2. Geographical Distribution of High-Impact, High-Tech Companies by Founder Nativity.

Table 5. High-Impact, High-Tech Companies by Founder Nativity and Employment (bivariate)

Employment	Native-Founded	Immigrant-Founded	TOTAL
Low Employment (1-4 employees)	175 (16.6%)	35 (17.1%)	210 (16.6%)
Medium Employment (5-20 employees)	633 (59.9%)	103 (50.2%)	736 (58.3%)
High Employment (>20 employees)	249 (23.6%)	67 (32.7%)	316 (25.0%)
TOTAL	1,057 100%)	205 (100%)	1,262 (100%)

Source: Corporate Research Board, High-Impact, *High-Tech Company Survey Database* (2009).
Note: Pearson chi-squared (2) = 8.48. P = 0.014.

Table 6. High-Impact, High-Tech Company Employment Regressed on Founder Nativity (multivariate w/controls)

Independent variables	Coefficient	P value
Founder Nativity	2.36	.83
Company Age	24.95	.07

Source: Corporate Research Board, *High-Impact, High-Tech Company Survey Database* (2009).
Note: Linear regression, sample weighted by age, sector, employment, and location. N = 1018. R-squared = .032. Dependent variable: company employment. Control variables (not displayed): 2-digit SIC, education level of most educated founder.

We measured technological performance in our survey by asking whether companies conducted R&D in their own labs, contracted out R&D, and held patents. Positive responses to these questions for the sample as a whole ranged from 17% for contract R&D to 27% for in-house R&D, with patent-holding lying in between at about 22% (Table 2). IFCs outperformed NFCs in bivariate tests on two of these three measures. About 36% of the IFCs maintained internal R&D labs, compared to 25% of the NFCs (Table 7). For patents, the difference was about the same, 29% for IFCs to 20% for NFCs (Table 8). Contract R&D was outsourced by the two groups of companies at roughly the same rate (Table 9).

Table 7. High-Impact, High-Tech Companies by Founder Nativity and Internal R&D

Internal R&D?	Native-Founded	Immigrant-Founded	TOTAL
Yes	263 (25.1%)	73 (36.1%)	336 (26.9%)
No	786 (74.9%)	129 (63.9%)	915 (73.1%)
TOTAL	1,049 (100%)	202 (100%)	1,251 (100%)

Source: Corporate Research Board, *High-Impact, High-Tech Company Survey Database* (2009).
Note: Pearson chi-squared (1) = 10.56. $P = 0.001$.

Table 8. High-Impact, High-Tech Companies by Founder Nativity and Patent-Holding

Patent?	Native-Founded	Immigrant-Founded	TOTAL
Yes	207 (20.4%)	55 (28.6%)	262 (21.8%)
No	805 (79.5%)	137 (71.3%)	942 (78.2%)
TOTAL	1,012 (100%)	192 (100%)	1,204 (100%)

Source: Corporate Research Board, High-Impact, *High-Tech Company Survey Database* (2009).
Note: Pearson chi-squared (1) = 6.36. $P = 0.012$.

Table 9. High-Impact, High-Tech Companies by Founder Nativity and Contract R&D

Contract R&D?	Native-Founded	Immigrant-Founded	TOTAL
Yes	167 (16.6%)	36 (18.9%)	203 (17.0%)
No	840 (83.4%)	154 (81.0%)	994 (83.0%)
TOTAL	1,007 (100%)	190 (100%)	1,197 (100%)

Source: Corporate Research Board, *High-Impact, High-Tech Company Survey Database* (2009).
Note: Pearson chi-squared (1) = 0.63. $P = 0.43$.

We conducted a variety of multivariate tests to explore how closely these variables, which are indicators of technological performance, are associated with founder nativity. Because the dependent variables here are binary (that is, they can only take on two values), we use a different set of statistical tools than in the analysis of economic performance, which is described above (Table 6). For instance, we use logistic regression, rather than ordinary least-squares regression. Viewed as a whole, our tests indicate that the relationship between founder nativity and technological performance is stronger than that between founder nativity and economic performance. However, this relationship falls short of statistical significance in our favored specification, which controls for company age, company employment, industry sector, and founder's level of education (Table 10).

IFCs are also about twice as likely as NFCs to report that they had a strategic relationship with a company outside the United States, such as a major supplier, key partner or major customer (Table 11). This bivariate relationship suggests that the cross-border social capital of foreign-born founders may be employed in building IFCs.

Of the 205 IFCs in the sample, more than half were founded only by foreign-born entrepreneurs – 85 by a single individual, 30 by a team of two, and five by teams of three or more (Table 12). About 55% of all companies in the sample were founded by a single individual (Table 2). We asked the rest of the companies about how the founders came together to create the company. Founding teams of companies with at least one foreign-born founder were slightly more likely to have gotten together through previous school or work relationships and slightly less likely to have done so through family relationships than founding teams made up only of U.S.-born founders (Table 13).

6.2. Profile of Immigrant Founders

We created a second database from our sample in which the unit of analysis is the individual founder, rather than the company. We obtained nativity data on 2,034 founders in total from our set of 1,415 companies. Of these, 261 are foreign-born, or about 12.8% (Table 14).

This share is very close to the current share of foreign-born in the U.S. population, which is about 12.6%, but smaller than the share of foreign-born in the science and engineering (S&E) graduate student population and the science, technology, engineering, and mathematics (STEM) workforce (Table 15).

The foreign-born share of all of these populations has grown rapidly over the past several decades. The 2000 Census found that 11.1% of the U.S. population was foreign born. In 1990, that figure was 7.9%, and it was 6.2% in 1980 (Figure 3). Among S&E graduate students, the foreign-born share was about 25% in 2005, up from 20% in 1985. And in the S&E workforce, the numbers show a rise to 16.7% in 2000, up from 8.2% in 1980 (Table 15).

Table 10. High-Impact, High-Tech Company Technological Performance Regressed on Founder Nativity (Multivariate W/Controls)

Independent Variables	Coefficient	P-value
Founder Nativity	0.75	0.69
Company Age	-0.0043	0.51
Company Employment	0.00045	0.31

Source: Corporate Research Board, *High-Impact, High-Tech Company Survey Database* (2009).
Note: Logistic regression, *weighted* by age, sector, employment, and location. N = 1012. Pseudo R-Squared = .10. Dependent variable: technological performance (dummy variable for positive response to any survey question on patenting, in-house R&D, or contract R&D). Control variables (not displayed): 2-digit SIC, education level of most educated founder.

Table 11. High-Impact, High-Tech Companies by Founder Nativity and Strategic Relationship with Company Outside United States

Foreign partner?	Native-Founded	Immigrant-Founded	TOTAL
Yes	238 (23.0%)	83 (41.9%)	321 (26.0%)
No	798 (77.0%)	115 (58.1%)	913 (74.0%)
TOTAL	1,036 (100%)	198 (100%)	1,234 (100%)

Source: Corporate Research Board, *High-Impact, High-Tech Company Survey Database* (2009).
Note: Pearson chi-squared (1) = 31.0. P = 0.000.

Table 12. Immigrant-Founded High-Impact, High-Tech Companies by Number of Founders and Founder Nativity

Number of Foreign-born Founders	Total number of founders in company						Number of Companies
	1	2	3	4	5	6	
1	85	52	14	5	3	1	160
2	0	30	4	3	0	1	38
3	0	0	4	1	0	0	5
5	0	0	0	0	2	0	2
Number of Companies	85	82	22	9	5	2	205

Source: Corporate Research Board, *High-Impact, High-Tech Company Survey Database* (2009).

Table 13. High-Impact, High-Tech Companies with Two or More Founders by Founder Nativity and How Founding Team Came Together

How founding team came together	Native-Founded	Native-Founded (%)	Immigrant-Founded	Immigrant-Founded (%)
Family	149	32.0	38	27.3
Attended school/college together	34	7.3	14	10.1
Worked together previously	166	35.6	57	41.0
Got together to start his business	65	13.9	15	10.8
Something else	40	8.6	9	6.5
More than one reason	12	2.6	6	4.3
TOTAL	**466**	**100**	**139**	**100**

Source: Corporate Research Board, *High-Impact, High-Tech Company Survey Database* (2009).

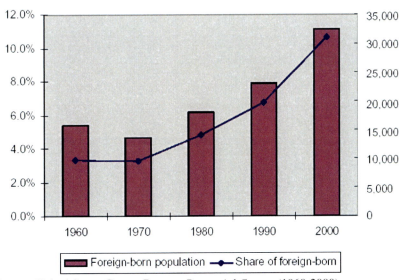

Source: United States Census Bureau, *Decennial Census* (1960-2000).

Figure 3. Foreign-Born Population of the United States (000s).

Table 14. Founders of High-Impact, High-Tech Companies by Nativity

	Number	Percentage
Native-born	1,773	87.2
Foreign-born	261	12.8
TOTAL	**2,034**	**100**

Source: Corporate Research Board, *High-Impact, High-Tech Company Survey Database* (2009).

Table 15. S&E Graduate Student Enrollment and Employment in STEM Occupations

S&E Graduate Student Enrollment			
Year	1985	1995	2005
Foreign-Born	79,940	102,885	146,696
Total	404,021	499,640	583,226
Foreign-Born Share	19.8%	20.6%	25.2%
Employment in STEM Occupations (in thousands)			
Year	1980	1990	2000
Foreign-Born	284	542	1,150
Total	3,459	5,046	6,871
Foreign-Born Share	8.2%	10.7%	16.7%

Source: NSB (2008) and Lowell and Regets (2006).

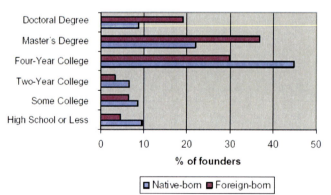

Source: Corporate Research Board, *High-Impact, High-Tech Company Survey Database* (2009).

Figure 4. Founders of High-Impact, High-Tech Companies by Nativity and Level of Education.

These earlier population estimates are the most relevant comparisons for this study, rather than the current estimate, because the vast majority of foreign-born founders were reported to have lived in the United States for decades. The average duration was more than a quarter-century, 25.9 years.

Only about 25% were reported to have been in the United States for less than 15 years (Table 16). About 77% of the foreign-born high-tech entrepreneurs in our sample are U.S. citizens (Table 17).

The foreign-born founders are a highly educated group. Roughly 55% of them hold a masters degree or doctorate. In fact, foreign-born founders are more than twice as likely as native-born founders to hold a doctorate and substantially more likely to hold a masters degree as well. On the other end of the spectrum, U.S.-born founders of high-impact, high-tech firms are about twice as likely as foreign born founders (9.5% versus 4.6%) to hold a high school degree or less (Table 18 and Figure 4).

Table 16. Foreign-Born Founders of High-Impact, High-Tech Companies by Duration of Stay in the United States

Percentile	Length of Stay (years)
25%	15
50%	25
75%	38
90%	50
95%	54
99%	60

Source: Corporate Research Board, *High-Impact, High-Tech Company Survey Database* (2009).
Note: N = 233. Mean = 25.9. Std. dev. = 16.3.

Table 17. Foreign-Born Founders of High-Impact, High-Tech Companies by U.S. Citizenship

U.S. Citizenship	Frequency	Percent
Yes	186	77.2
No	55	22.8
TOTAL	**241**	**100**

Source: Corporate Research Board, *High-Impact, High-Tech Company Survey Database* (2009).

Table 18. Founders of High-Impact, High-Tech Companies by Nativity and Level of Education

Level of Education	Native-born	Foreign-born	TOTAL
High School Degree or Less	154	10	**164**
%	9.5	4.6	**8.9**
Some College	139	14	**153**
%	8.6	6.4	**8.3**
Two Year College/Technical Degree	107	7	**114**
%	6.6	3.2	**6.2**
Four Year College Degree	724	65	**789**
%	44.7	29.9	**42.9**
Master's Degree	356	80	**436**
%	22.0	36.9	**23.7**
Doctoral/Professional Degree	141	41	**182**
%	8.7	18.9	9.9
TOTAL	**1,621**	**217**	**1,838**

Source: Corporate Research Board, High-Impact, *High-Tech Company Survey Database* (2009).

Table 19. Foreign-Born Founders of High-Impact, High-Tech Companies by Location of Highest Degree

Highest Education in U.S.?	Frequency	Percent
Yes	148	66.7
No	74	33.3
TOTAL	**222**	**100**

Source: Corporate Research Board, *High-Impact, High-Tech Company Survey Database* (2009).

Exactly two-thirds of the foreign-born founders about whom we have information received their highest level of education in the United States (Table 19).

The countries of origin of the foreign-born founders are diverse. Fifty-four countries are represented in our founder database – about 28% of the United Nations' membership. India is the largest source country, accounting for about 16% of this group. The U.K. provided 10%, followed by Canada and Japan, each of which constituted 6%, and Germany, which accounted for 5%. China and Cuba were the home countries of about 3%. To China's total, one might add Hong Kong and Taiwan, which bring it up to a third-place tie with Canada and Japan. All of the inhabited continents and major world regions are represented in the group. Table 20 lists the countries of origin, and they are broken down by region in Figure 5.

Table 20. Foreign-Born Founders of High-Impact, High-Tech Companies by Country of Origin

Country	Number	Percent	Country	Number	Percent
India	40	15.9	Haiti	2	0.8
UK	25	10.0	Holland	2	0.8
Canada	15	6.0	Iraq	2	0.8
China	15	6.0	Jamaica	2	0.8
Japan	15	6.0	Philippine	2	0.8
Germany	13	5.2	Serbia	2	0.8
Cuba	8	3.2	Sweden	2	0.8
Iran	7	2.8	West Indies	2	0.8
Russia	7	2.8	Argentina	1	0.4
France	6	2.4	Burma	1	0.4
Mexico	5	2.0	Chile	1	0.4
Vietnam	5	2.0	Colombia	1	0.4
Australia	4	1.6	Croatia	1	0.4
Belgium	4	1.6	Denmark	1	0.4
Ireland	4	1.6	El Salvador	1	0.4
Korea	4	1.6	Ghana	1	0.4
Pakistan	4	1.6	Guyana	1	0.4
Ukraine	4	1.6	Israel	1	0.4
Austria	3	1.2	Nicaragua	1	0.4
Brazil	3	1.2	Nigeria	1	0.4
Italy	3	1.2	Panama	1	0.4
Lebanon	3	1.2	Peru	1	0.4
Netherlands	3	1.2	Poland	1	0.4
Romania	3	1.2	Spain	1	0.4
South Africa	3	1.2	Tanzania	1	0.4
Switzerland	3	1.2	Turkey	1	0.4
Greece	2	0.8	Uruguay	1	0.4

Source: Corporate Research Board, *High-Impact, High-Tech Company Survey Database* (2009).

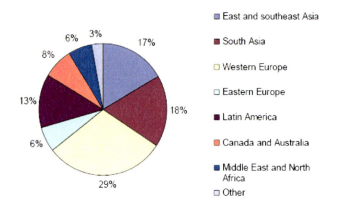

Source: Corporate Research Board, *High-Impact, High-Tech Company Survey Database* (2009).

Figure 5. Foreign-Born Founders of High-Impact, High-Tech Companies by Region of Origin.

6.3. Gender and Race of Founders

We asked respondents about the gender of all founders and the race of U.S.-born founders (using the standard categories of the U.S. Census). About 22% of all the high-tech HICs in our sample included at least one woman in their founding teams. The founding teams of IFCs were statistically significantly more likely to include at least one woman; about 30% did so, compared to about 20% of NFCs (Table 21).

Table 21. High-Impact, High-Tech Companies by Founder Nativity and Gender

	Native-Founded	Immigrant-Founded	TOTAL
All Male Founders	824 (79.4%)	142 (69.9%)	966 (77.9%)
At Least One Female Founder	213 (20.5%)	61 (30.0%)	274 (22.1%)
TOTAL	1,037 (100%)	203 (100%)	1,240 (100%)

Source: Corporate Research Board, *High-Impact, High-Tech Company Survey Database* (2009).
Note: Pearson chi-squared (1) = 8.92. P = 0.003.

About 15% of all the founders of the high-tech HICs in our sample are female. The female founders are distributed similarly by nativity to all founders, that is, females constitute about the same share of U.S.-born founders as of foreign-born founders (Table 22). Male foreign-born founders are more likely to team up with women, regardless of nativity, than male native-born founders (Table 23). Although the absolute numbers are very small, we find a similar pattern in the data on teams that include U.S. minorities. Foreign-born founders are more likely to team up with U.S. minority founders than are native-born white founders (Table 24).

Table 22. Founders of High-Impact, High-Tech Companies by Founder Nativity and Gender

	Native-born Founder	Foreign-born Founder	TOTAL
Male	1,503	218	**1,721**
%	85.3	83.8	**85.1**
Female	259	42	**301**
%	14.7	16.1	**14.9**
TOTAL	**1,762**	**260**	**2,022**

Source: Corporate Research Board, *High-Impact, High-Tech Company Survey Database* (2009).

Table 23. High-Impact, High-Tech Companies by Founder Nativity and Gender in Companies with More than One Founder

	All Founders Male	At Least One Female Founder	TOTAL
All Male Founders Native-born	271	156	**426**
%	63.5	36.5	**100**
At Least One Male Founder Foreign-born	58	41	**100**
%	58.6	41.4	**100**
TOTAL	**329**	**197**	**526**

Source: Corporate Research Board, *High-Impact, High-Tech Company Survey Database* (2009).

Table 24. High-Impact, High-Tech Companies by Founder Nativity and Race of Native-Born Founders in Companies with More than One Founder

	All Founders Are White or Foreign-born	At Least One Minority Founder	TOTAL
Native-founded Companies with at Least One White Founder	370	23	**393**
%	94.1	5.9	**100**
Immigrant-founded Companies with at Least One Native-born Founder	55	12	**67**
%	82.1	17.9	**100**
TOTAL	**425**	**35**	**457**

Source: Corporate Research Board, *High-Impact, High-Tech Company Survey Database* (2009).

U.S. minorities constitute about 6% of all founders. Hispanic or Latino founders are the most commonly represented group, accounting for 2% of all founders, followed by African Americans, Asian Americans, and American Indians in that order. U.S. minorities represent about 15% of the native-born founders of IFCs, compared to about 5% of the founders of NFCs (Table 25). Here, too, the small absolute number (15 U.S. minority individuals out of 102 native-born individuals who were included in the founding teams of IFCs) makes generalization hazardous.

The higher likelihood of foreign-born founders to team up with female and U.S. minority founders is intriguing, small sample size notwithstanding. The gender variation might be accounted for by marriage if foreign-born male founders are more likely to go into business with their native-born spouses than native-born male founders are. The minority variation might be accounted for by co-ethnicity between foreign- and native-born founders. These findings provide hypotheses for further research with larger sample sizes.

Table 25. Native-Born Founders of High-Impact, High-Tech Companies by Race and Company Type

	Native-Founded Company	Immigrant-Founded Company	TOTAL
American Indian or Alaska Native	14	2	**16**
%	0.9	2.0	**1.0**
Asian	15	3	**18**
%	1.0	2.9	**1.1**
Black or African American	25	1	**26**
%	1.6	1.0	**1.6**
Hispanic or Latino	24	8	**32**
%	1.6	7.8	**2.0**
Native Hawaiian or Other Pacific Islander	4	1	**5**
%	0.3	1.0	**0.3**
All U.S. Minorities	82	15	**97**
%	5.4	14.7	**6.0**
White	1,445	87	**1,532**
%	94.6	85.3	**94.0**
TOTAL	**1,527**	**102**	**1,629**
%	**100**	**100**	**100**

Source: Corporate Research Board, *High-Impact, High-Tech Company Survey Database* (2009).

7.0. RESEARCH AND POLICY AGENDA

Our study quantifies the role of foreign-born founders involved in high-tech entrepreneurship by examining a nationally representative sample of rapidly growing high-impact companies. In this section, we briefly identify some of the key policy issues that relate to our study's findings. We also describe a future agenda for research in this area.

7.1. Key Policy Issues

One important set of issues illuminated by this study involves the linkages among non-immigrant visa categories and between non-immigrant status and legal permanent residence. A large proportion of the immigrant founders in our sample found their way from higher education to professional work to the green card and, ultimately, citizenship. They gained sufficient certainty about their immigration status during this journey that they were willing to make the investment of a lifetime by starting their own businesses. It is possible that some potential high-tech entrepreneurs who are admitted in a non-immigrant status get trapped in that status without sufficient reason. Even those individuals who have a reasonable prospect of extending their stay in the United States may lack the certainty that they will be here long enough to be able to reap the benefits of taking the entrepreneurial "leap," because of the way the immigration system handles their cases. As a result, they never take the leap, and their potential entrepreneurial contribution to the nation may be lost.

The adjustment process by which a visa holder moves from one status to another is often slow and cumbersome, and it has gotten harder in some respects in recent years. Admission as a student is generally not too difficult, as long as the applicant has an offer of a place from a credible school and the means to pay (Lowell et al. 2007). However, the adjustment from student status to non-immigrant work status is strewn with obstacles. In many cases, recent graduates can stay for an additional year after graduation without changing status if they are employed in "optional practical training" (OPT) directly related to their field of study. OPT was recently extended to 29 months for graduates in STEM fields (*Migration News* 2008). However, if the student visa holder is without a firm job offer from a sponsor who holds a non-immigrant visa slot when the OPT period expires, the former student must leave the country immediately (as he or she must upon graduation as well if not eligible for OPT).

The availability of non-immigrant employment visa slots to graduating students and employers who desire them is uncertain. As we noted in section 2, the H-1B category, which is the largest one for long-term non-immigrant workers, has faced a glut of applicants for a limited number of visas in recent years. These visas are distributed primarily through a lottery, and no priorities are set with respect to the types of qualifications that the country might value beyond the general language of the law. Applicants are left in the dark for many months and sometimes years as to whether they will be admitted.

Indeed, it was this uncertainty, the so-called H-1B "cap gap," that seems to have stimulated the extension of OPT described above (U.S.I.C.E. 2009). Yet, this fix simply expands the pool of H-1B applicants who are in limbo. The second largest long-term non-immigrant work visa category, the L-1 for intra-company transferees, is increasingly subject to similar uncertainty as companies have apparently begun to use it to try to work around the constraints of the H-1B process (Economic Policy Institute 2007).

The third step along this pathway, from temporary work status to the green card, is perhaps the most difficult of all. Unless the aspiring immigrant marries an American citizen and thus becomes eligible for legal permanent residence as a member of a citizen's family, the wait can be quite long and burdened with onerous conditions and uncertainty. The conditions include remaining with the sponsoring employer until the green card has been approved. The wait for an employment-based green card usually lasts several years, and it is often much longer. The July 2009 *Department of State Visa Bulletin*, for instance, shows that green cards are now being processed for applicants who filed their initial forms as far back as 2000. Because green cards are subject to annual per-country limits, applicants from India, China, Mexico, and the Philippines, which are among the largest source countries, must usually wait longer than applicants from other countries.

Although immigration policy is a domain of exclusive federal competence in the United States,[12] state and local actors may play constructive roles in shaping a federal policy that supports technology-based economic development. The Greater Cleveland Partnership, for instance, has recently called for the federal government to establish high-skill immigration zones in distressed metropolitan areas (Greater Cleveland Partnership, 2009). Such calls are natural extensions of policies that focus on attraction of entrepreneurial talent at the regional, state, and local levels.

7.2. Areas for Further Research

This study and related work on high-tech immigrant entrepreneurship leaves open many questions. Three areas for further research strike us as particularly interesting to pursue. The first and most fundamental of these areas is whether native-born and foreign-born high-tech entrepreneurs are substitutes or complements. Do the foreign-born exploit opportunities that, in their absence, native-born entrepreneurs would have recognized and exploited, or are these opportunities generated by their presence? The evidence in other areas of immigration is ambiguous (Card 2005, Fairlie and Meyer 2003, Light and Rosenstein 1995). Even a high rate of high-tech immigrant entrepreneurship, such as that found by Saxenian (1999) in Silicon Valley, does not necessarily indicate that immigrants and natives are complements, rather than substitutes. And, of course, we cannot re-run history to explore the counterfactual in which the border is closed. However, carefully controlled comparative research designs may help us move closer to the elusive answer to this question.

The second area of interest is closely related to the first: do IFCs and NFCs follow similar strategies and operate similarly? If the two groups of companies tend to pursue different opportunities, as implied by the complementarity hypothesis, we should be able to observe differences in their business models and value chains. IFCs, for example, may export more aggressively than NFCs and tailor their products accordingly. Our finding that IFCs are more likely than NFCs to report that they had strategic relationship with a company outside the United States is an intriguing bit of evidence, but it requires much more substantiation before broader claims can be made with respect to this issue. This agenda would also lead naturally toward an exploration of the causes of such differences, such as differences in the life experiences and social networks of the companies' founders.

The final research agenda that we highlight centers on the regional impacts of high-tech immigrant entrepreneurship. Economic growth and migration both exhibit geographical agglomeration. Industrial clusters rise and fall, and with them, the cities (such as Detroit or Hollywood) with which these clusters are associated. Immigrants, too, tend to cluster as ethnic communities grow in gateway cities like New York, Los Angeles, and Miami. The study of high-tech immigrant entrepreneurship should allow us to link these two phenomena together. This study reveals that high-tech immigrant entrepreneurs are distributed much like the immigrant population as a whole, but our sample is not large enough to explore the economic consequences at the regional level. Comparative regional studies would shed light on these fascinating issues. The apparent propensity of immigrants to team up with U.S.-born women and minorities might also be studied in this context.

8.0. CONCLUSION

Immigrants play an important role in founding high-impact, high-tech companies in the United States. This group of companies is very important to the nation, because it accounts for a disproportionate share of job creation and economic growth. About 16% of the companies in our nationally representative sample count at least one immigrant among their founders.

High-impact, high-tech companies founded by immigrant entrepreneurs and those founded by native-born entrepreneurs are similar in many ways. They operate in the same industries and are about the same size. One important difference is their location. Immigrant-founded companies tend to be located in states that have large immigrant populations. Another difference is that immigrant-founded companies in our sample are about twice as likely to have a strategic relationship with a foreign firm, such as a major supplier, key partner, or major customer. Immigrant-founded companies may also have a higher level of technological performance. Of the immigrant-founded companies in our sample, for instance, 36% conducted R&D, compared to 25% of the native-founded companies, and 29% held patents, compared to 20% of the native-founded companies. However, when control variables are included in the analysis, the association between immigrant founding and these technological variables becomes statistically insignificant.

The immigrant high-tech entrepreneurs in our sample are deeply rooted in the United States. A large proportion of them have been in this country for two decades or more. More than three-quarters of them are U.S. citizens. Two-thirds of them received undergraduate or graduate degrees in this country. The 250 foreign-born entrepreneurs on whom we have data hail from 54 countries in all regions of the world. India is the largest source country, accounting for 16% of this group, followed by the U.K. at 10%.

Policymakers are rightly concerned that government sustains a healthy climate for starting and running high-impact companies like those in our sample. Immigration policy, as it affects highly educated and highly experienced foreign-born individuals who might be drawn into high-tech entrepreneurship, is an important element of that climate. This element deserves more attention and more creative thinking than it has received in the past.

BIBLIOGRAPHY

Acs, Z. J. & Audretsch, D. B. (1990). *Innovation and small firms. Cambridge.* MIT Press.

Acs, Z. J., Audretsch, D. B. & Strom, R. J. (2009). Entrepreneurship, growth, and public policy. New York: Cambridge University Press.

Acs, Z. J. & Mueller, P. (2008). Employment effects of business dynamics: mice, gazelles, and elephants. *Small Business Economics, 30*, 85-100.

Acs, Z. J., Parsons, W. & Tracy, S. (2008). High impact firms: Gazelles revisited. SBA Office of Advocacy Working Paper no. 328. Washington: SBA.

Acs, Z. J., Audretsch, D. B., Braunerhjelm, P. & Carlsson, B. (2005). The knowledge spillover theory of entrepreneurship. Discussion Papers on Entrepreneurship, Growth and Public Policy No. 27. Jena: Max Planck Institute of Economics.

Anderson, Stuart, and Michaela Platzer. (2006). American made. Washington: National Venture Capital Association.

Arrow, K. J. (1962). Economic welfare and the allocation of resources for invention. In: The rate and direction of inventive activity (pp. 609-626). Princeton: Princeton University Press.

Andrescu, T., et al. (2008). Cross-cultural analysis of students with exceptional talent in mathematical problem solving. *Notices of the AMS., 55*, 1248-1260.

Autio, E. (2005). Global entrepreneurship monitor 2005 report on high expectation entrepreneurship. Wellesley: *Babson College.*

Bates, T. & Dunham, C. (1993). Asian American success in self-employment. *Economic Development Quarterly, 7*, 199-214.

Baumol, W. J., Litan, R. E. & Schramm, C. J. (2007). Good capitalism, bad capitalism, and the economics of growth and prosperity. *New Haven*: Yale University Press.

Bhattacharjee, Y. 13 April (2007). Study finds foreign high-tech workers earn less. *Science, 316*, 184.

Bhide, A. (2008). *The venturesome economy.* Princeton: Princeton University Press.

Borjas, G. J. (1990). *Friends or strangers?* New York: Basic Books.

Borjas, G. J. (1999). *Heaven's door: Immigration policy and the American economy.* Princeton: Princeton University Press.

Borjas, G. J. (2005). The labor market impact of high-skill immigration," NBER Working Paper No. 11217. Cambridge: NBER.

Brush (2003). In Hart, D.M., (Ed.), *The emergence of entrepreneurship policy* (pp. 141-154). New York: Cambridge University Press.

Bullvaag, E., et al. (2006). *Global entrepreneurship monitor, national entrepreneurship assessment*, U.S.A., 2004-2005 executive report. Wellesley: Babson College.

Burton, M. D. (1995). The emergence and evolution of employment systems in high-technology firms. Ph.D. dissertation, Department of Sociology, Stanford University.

Card, D. (2005). *Is the new immigration really so bad*? NBER Working Paper No. 11547. Cambridge: NBER.

Carlsson, B. & Jacobson, S. (1997). Diversity creation and technological systems: A technology policy perspective. In Edquist, C., (Ed.), *Systems of innovation* (266- 294). London: Pinter.

Christensen, C. M. & Rosenbloom, R. S. (1995). Explaining the attacker's advantage: Technological paradigms, organizational dynamics, and the value network. *Research Policy, 24*, 233-257.

Clarke, S. E. & Gaile, G. L. (1989). Moving toward entrepreneurial economic development policies: Opportunities and barriers. *Policy Studies Journal, 17*, 574-598.

Cuno Engineering Corp. v.Automatic Devices Corp. (1941). 314 US 84.

DesRoches, D., et al. (2007). *Kauffman firm survey: Baseline methodology report*. Princeton: Mathematica Research.

Economic Policy Institute. (2007). *Outsourcing America's technology and knowledge jobs*. Briefing Paper #187. Washington: EPI.

Eisinger, P. K. (1988). *The rise of the entrepreneurial state*. Madison: University of Wisconsin Press.

EurActiv. 21 December 2008. An EU blue card program for highly-skilled immigrants? Available at http://www.euractiv.com/en/socialeurope/eu-blue-card-high-skilledimmigrants/article-170986, accessed April 13, 2009.

Fairlie, R. W. (2008). *Estimating the contribution of immigrant business owners to the U.S. economy*. Office of Advocacy Research Summary No. 334. Washington: Small Business Administration.

Fairlie, R. W. & Meyer, B. D. (2003). The effect of immigration on native self-employment. *Journal of Labor Economics, 21*, 619-650.

Federman, M. N., Harrington, D. E. & Krynski, K. J. (2006). Vietnamese manicurists: Are immigrants displacing natives or finding new nails to polish? *Industrial and Labor Relations Review, 59*, 302-317.

Florida, R. (2003). *The rise of the creative class*. New York: Basic.
Florida, R. (2005). *The flight of the creative class*. New York: HarperBusiness.
Galbraith, J. K. (1952). *American capitalism*. Boston: Houghton-Mifflin.
Graham, O. L. (1992). *Losing time: The industrial policy debate*. Cambridge: Harvard University Press.
Greater Cleveland Partnership. 5 March (2009). 2009/2010 public policy agenda. Available at http://www.gcpartnership.com/News.aspx?id=3196, accessed April, *10*, 2009.
Griliches, Z. (1958). Research costs and social returns: Hybrid corn and related innovations. *Journal of Political Economy, 66*, 419-431.
Hadlock, P., Hecker, D. & Gannon, J. (1991). High technology employment: another view. *Monthly Labor Review*, July, 26-30.
Haltiwanger, J. (2009). Entrepreneurship and job growth. In Acs, Z.J., Audretsch, D. B. & Strom, R. J. (Eds.), *Entrepreneurship, economic growth, and public policy* (119- 145). New York: Cambridge University Press.
Hannan, M. T., Burton, M. D. & Baron, J. M. (1996). Inertia and change in the early years: Employment relations in young, high technology firms. *Industrial and Corporate Change* 5:503-536.
Hart, D. M. (1998). *Forged consensus: science, technology, and economic policy in the United States, 1921-1953*. Princeton: Princeton University Press.
Hart, D. M. (2006). Global flows of talent: Benchmarking the U.S. Washington: Information Technology and Innovation Foundation.
Hart, D. M. Forthcoming. The social context for high-potential entrepreneurship in the U.S.: An historical-institutional perspective. In Bird, A. (Ed.), *Entrepreneurship in Japan, China, and the U.S.* Montreal: McGill University Press.
Henrekson, M. & Johansson, D. (2008). Gazelles as job creators. IFN Working Paper No. 733. Stockholm: IFN.
Hsu, D. H. & Kenney, M. (2005). Organizing venture capital: the rise and demise of American Research & Development Corporation, 1946–1973. *Industrial and Corporate Change, 14*, 579-616.
Hsu, D. H., Roberts, E. B. & Eesley, C. E. (2007). Entrepreneurs from technology-based universities: Evidence from MIT. *Research Policy, 36*, 768-788.
Hughes, K. H. (2005). *Building the next American century*. Washington: Woodrow Wilson Center Press.

Hunt, J. & Gauthier-Loiselle, M. (2008). *How much does immigration boost innovation?* NBER Working Paper No. 14312. Cambridge: NBER.

Institute of International Education. (2008). *Open doors 2008.* Washington: IIE.

Ionescu, Dina. (2006). *Engaging diasporas as development partners for home and destination countries.* Geneva: International Organization for Migration.

Kenney, M. (Ed.) (2000). *Understanding silicon valley.* Stanford: Stanford University Press.

Kerr, W. R. & Lincoln, W. F. (2008). The supply side of innovation: H-1B visa reforms and U.S. ethnic inventions. Harvard Business School Working Paper No. 09-005. Boston: HBS.

Kierkegaard, J. F. (2007). *The accelerating decline in America's high-skill workforce.* Policy Analyses in International Economics No. 84. Washington: Peterson Institute.

Kirzner, I. M. (1973). *Competition and entrepreneurship.* Chicago: University of Chicago Press.

Koser, K. (2007). *International migration: A very short introduction.* New York: Oxford University Press.

Kuznetsov, Y. & Sabel, C. (2006). International migration of talent, diaspora networks, and development. In Kuznetsov, Y., (Ed.), *Diaspora networks and the international migration of skills* (3-20). Washington: World Bank Institute.

Lentz, B. F. & Laband, D. N. (1990). Entrepreneurial success and occupational inheritance among proprietors. *Canadian Journal of Economics, 23*, 563-579.

Levin, S. G., et al. (2004). Differential employment patterns for citizens and non-citizens in science and engineering in the U.S. *Growth and Change, 3 5*, 456-475.

Light, I. H. & Gold, S. J. (2000). *Ethnic economies.* San Diego: Academic Press.

Light, I. H. & Rosenstein, C. N. (1995). *Race, ethnicity, and entrepreneurship in urban America.* New York: Aldine de Gruyter.

Lowell, B. L. (2006). *Projected numbers of foreign computer and engineering workers under the Senate's Comprehensive Immigration Reform Act (S. 2611).* Washington: Institute for the Study of International Migration.

Lowell, B. L., Bump, M. & Martin, S. (2007). *Foreign students coming to America.* Washington: Institute for the Study of International Migration.

Lowell, B. L. & Salzman, H. (2007). *Into the eye of the storm: Assessing the evidence on science and engineering education, quality, and workforce demand.* Washington: Urban Institute.

Lowell, B. L. & Regets, M. (2006). A half-century snapshot of the STEM workforce, 1950 to 2000. Commission on Professionals in Science and Technology STEM Workforce Data Project White Paper No. 1. Washington: CPST.

Lucas, R. E. (1988). On the mechanics of economic development. *Journal of Monetary Economics, 22*, 3-42.

McCraw, T. K. (2007). *Prophet of innovation.* Cambridge: Harvard University Press. Mervis, J. 3 April 2009. Newsmaker interview: Nancy Pelosi. *Science, 324*, 24.

Migration News. April 2008. H-1B, labor. 14(2), available on-line at http://migration.ucdavis.edu/mn.

Monti, D. J., Smith-Doerr, L. & MacQuaid, J. (2007). *Immigrant entrepreneurs in the Massachusetts biotechnology industry.* Boston: Immigrant Learning Center.

National Academy of Sciences. (2005). *Rising above the gathering storm.* Washington: National Academies Press.

National Governors Association, Center for Best Practices. 2006. *Enhancing competitiveness.* Washington: NGA.

National Science Board. (2008). *Science and Engineering Indicators 2008.* Washington: NSB.

Nelson, R. R. (1959). The simple economics of basic scientific research. *Journal of Political Economy, 67*, 297-312.

Osborne, D. E. (1988). *Laboratories of democracy.* Boston: Harvard Business School Press.

Ottaviano, G. I. P. & Peri, G. (2006). Rethinking the effects of immigration on wages. NBER Working Paper No. 12497.

Ottaviano, G. I. P. & Peri, G. (2007). The economic value of cultural diversity: Evidence from U.S. cities. *Journal of Economic Geography, 6*, 9-44.

Pages, E., Freedman, D. & Von Bargen, P. (2003). Entrepreneurship as a state and local economic development strategy. In D.M. Hart (Ed.), *The emergence of entrepreneurship policy* (pp. 240-259). New York: Cambridge University Press.

Peters, A. H. & Fisher, P. (2004). The failures of economic development incentives. *Journal of the American Planning Association., 70*, 27-37.

Portes, A., Guarnizo, L. E. & Haller, W. J. (2002). Transnational entrepreneurs: An alternative form of immigrant economic adaptation. *American Sociological Review, 67*, 278-298.

Reynolds, P. D. & Curtin, R. T. (2007). Business creation in the United States in 2006: Panel study of entrepreneurial dynamics II. Unpublished manuscript.

Romer, P. M. (1990). Endogenous technological change. *Journal of Political Economy, 98*, S71- 102.

Ruttan, V. W. (2001). *Technology, growth, and development.* New York: Oxford University Press.

Saxenian, A. (1999). *Silicon valley's new immigrant entrepreneurs.* San Francisco: Public Policy Institute of California.

Saxenian, A. (2006). *The new Argonauts.* Cambridge: Harvard University Press.

Scherer, F. M. (1984). *Innovation and growth: Schumpeterian perspectives.* Cambridge: MIT Press.

Scherer, F. M. (1992). *International high-technology competition.* Cambridge: Harvard University Press.

Schumpeter, J. A. (1942). *Capitalism, socialism, and democracy.* New York: Harper.

Shane, S. A. (2008). *The illusions of entrepreneurship: The costly myths that entrepreneurs, investors, and policy makers live by.* New Haven: Yale University Press.

Shane, S. & Venktaraman, S. (2000). The promise of entrepreneurship as a field of research. *Academy of Management Review, 25*, 217-226.

Skills Research Initiative. (2008). *International mobility of highly-skilled workers.* Ottawa: Industry Canada and Human Resources and Social Development Canada.

Solow, R. M. (1957). Technical change and the aggregate production function. *Review of Economics and Statistics, 39*, 312-320.

U.S. Immigration and Customs Enforcement (U.S. I.C.E.). March 2009. Fact sheet: Information for employers on the cap-gap extension of optional practical training. Washington: U.S. I.C.E.

U.S. Small Business Administration, Office of Advocacy. 2007. *The Small Business Economy for Data Year 2006: A Report to the President.* Washington: U.S. Government Printing Office.

Utterback, J. M. (1994). *Mastering the dynamics of innovation.* Boston: Harvard Business School Press.

Varga, A. (1998). *University research and regional innovation.* Boston: Kluwer.

Wadhwa, V., et al. (2007ᵃ). *Intellectual property, the immigration backlog, and reverse brain drain.* Durham: Duke University School of Engineering.

Wadhwa, V., et al. (2007b). *America's new immigrant entrepreneurs.* Durham: Duke University School of Engineering.

Waits, M. J. (2000). Economic development strategies in the American states. *International Journal of Public Administration, 23*,1541-1571.

Wessner, C. W. (2007). *An assessment of the SBIR program.* Washington: National Academies Press.

Wong, P. K., Ho, Y. P. & Autio, E. (2005). Entrepreneurship, innovation, and economic growth: Evidence from GEM data. *Small Business Economics, 24*, 335-350.

APPENDIX 1. HIGH-TECHNOLOGY SICS (3 DIGIT)

As noted in the main text of this report, our definition of high-technology draws primarily on the Bureau of Labor Statistics' definition, which uses R&D *employment* as a share of total employment as the key criterion, as described by Hadlock, Hecker, and Gannon (1991). Industries in which R&D employment as a share of total employment is 50% greater than the industry average are included in the BLS definition. We dropped SIC 874, management and public relations, which met the BLS definition, but which has a far larger number of firms in it than any other industry and therefore would have skewed our results toward that industry. We also added several other SICs that have a high ratio of R&D *spending* to total revenues, which are identified in Varga (1998). Our final list of high-tech sectors is very similar to that used by the Kauffman Firm Survey (DesRoches *et al.* 2007, 27).

Manufacturing	SIC
Crude petroleum and natural gas	131
Cigarettes	211
Miscellaneous textile goods	229
Pulp mills	261
Miscellaneous converted paper products	267
Industrial inorganic chemicals	281

Plastic materials and synthetics	282
Medicinals and botanicals	283
Soap	284
Paints	285
Industrial organic chemicals	286
Agricultural chemicals	287
Miscellaneous chemical products	289
Petroleum refining	291
Miscellaneous petroleum and coal products	299
Reclaimed rubber	303
Nonferrous rolling and drawing	335
Ordnance and accessories, not elsewhere classified	348
Engines and turbines	351
Construction and related machinery	353
Metalworking machinery	354
Special industry machinery	355
General industrial machinery	356
Computer and office equipment	357
Industrial machines, not elsewhere classified	359
Electronic distribution equipment	361
Electrical industrial apparatus	362
Household appliances	363
Electric lighting and wiring	364
Audio and video equipment	365
Communications equipment	366
Electronic components and accessories	367
Miscellaneous electrical equipment and supplies	369
Motor vehicles and equipment	371
Aircraft and parts	372
Railroads	374
Guided missiles and space	376
Miscellaneous transportation equipment	379
Search and navigation equipment	381
Measuring and controlling devices	382
Optical instruments and lenses	383
Medical instruments and supplies	384
Ophthalmic goods	385
Photographic equipment and supplies	386

(Continued)	
Manufacturing	**SIC**
Services	
Communication services, not elsewhere classified	489
Computer and data processing services 737	737
Engineering and architectural services	871
Research and development and testing services	873
Services, not elsewhere classified	899

APPENDIX 2. QUESTIONNAIRE

OMB CONTROL NUMBER: 3245-0364
EXPIRATION DATE: 08/31/2011

Hello, have I reached [Business Name]?

Yes	1
No [okay, thank you]	2

Is this a non-profit organization?
[Ask only if this name appears to be a non-profit, such as a university, school, hospital, etc.]

No	1
Yes [okay, thank you for your time]	2
Not asked	3
Don't know	8
Refused	9

I'm calling from George Mason University. Can you put me through to [Name]'s office?

Not available	1
Yes	2
This is him/her	3
No one here by that name, no longer works here, etc.	4
No/refuse	5

Perhaps there is someone else I can speak with. I'm calling from George Mason University. I'm working on a research project and we would like to ask a few questions of someone who knows about the founding and history of [Business Name]. We are not asking for any financial information.

No one can do this *[offer to call back at a specific time]*	1
Put through to potential respondent	2

Hi. Is this the office of [Name] or [Name] him/herself?

No	1
Yes	2

I'm calling from George Mason University. We are working on a research project supported by the Small Business Administration of the U.S. government. We are studying the role of high-growth companies in the American economy. For the study, we would like to speak for a few minutes with someone who knows about the founding and history of [Business Name]. Are you knowledgeable about that? We are not asking for any financial information.

Yes	1
No	2

[I'm calling from George Mason University]. I'm working on a research project supported by the Small Business Administration of the US government. For this study, we would like to speak for a few minutes with someone who knows about the founding and history of this company. Can you suggest someone? We are not asking for any financial information.

Yes— transfer	1
Yes—person on the phone	2
No *[code as soft refusal, unless respondent says not to call back]*	3

Can you suggest someone else?

Yes	1
No	2

[I'm calling from George Mason University]. We are working on a research project supported by the Small Business Administration of the U.S. government. For this study, we would like to speak for a few minutes with someone who knows about the founding and history of this company. Are you knowledgeable about that? We are not asking for any financial information.

Yes	1
No	2

OK, great. Before I ask the questions, I want to let you know that they will only take about 5 to 10 minutes to answer. Participation in this study is voluntary and you can skip any questions you choose not to answer. Responses will be kept confidential and the names of businesses or individuals will not be published.

What is your job title?

In what city or county is the company's headquarters located?

In what state?

In what country?

What industry would you say your firm is part of?

[If the respondent is not sure, probe: For example, is your company involved with pharmaceuticals, aircraft, software, industrial equipment, computer equipment, engineering, or something else?]

What year was this business founded? *[Enter 4-digit year]*

[If no response] **Was it:**

Before 1980	1
1980 to 1989	2
1990 to 1999	3
2000 or later	4
Don't know	8
Refused	9

Is the company publicly traded or privately held?

Publicly traded	1
Privately held	2
Something else	3
Don't know	8
Refused	9

Does the company have a research and development division or laboratory?

Yes	1
No	2
Don't know	8
Refused	9

Does it support R&D projects elsewhere, such as at a university or contract research firm?

Yes	1
No	2
Don't know	8
Refused	9

Does the company hold any patents or have patent applications pending?

Yes	1
No	2
Don't know	8
Refused	9

Does the company have a strategic relationship with any firms outside the U.S.? That would include foreign firms that are major suppliers, key partners or major customers.

Yes	1
No	2
Don't know	8
Refused	9

Now I have some questions about the founder or founders of this company. How many individuals would you identify as founders?

[DEFINITION: a founder is the person or people who owned part of the firm when it first began to cover all salaries and wages].

We would like to get information on the 5 most important founders.
Can you please provide their first names?
What is the first person's name?
What is the 2nd person's name?
What is the 3rd person's name?
What is the 4th person's name?
What is the 5th person's name?
OK, for [Founder 1], that is a man (woman) correct?

Male	1
Female	2
Don't know	8
Refused	9

Can you tell me if he/she was born in the U.S. or somewhere else?
[DEFINITION: U.S. includes Puerto Rico, Guam, etc. and territories]

U.S.	1
Somewhere else	2
Don't know	8
Refused	9

What country was that?

About how many years has he/she lived in the U.S.?
[If deceased: About how many years was he/she in the U.S. when he/she passed away?]
Is he/she now a U.S. citizen?

Yes	1
No	2
Don't know	8
Refused	9

What is his/her highest level of education? Would you say high school or less, some college, two-year college or technical degree, four-year college degree, Master's degree or doctoral/professional degree?

High school degree or less	1
Some college	2
Two year college or technical degree	3
Four year college degree	4
Master's degree	5
Doctoral/professional degree	6
Don't know	8
Refused	9

Was the most recent education obtained in the U.S.?

Yes	1
No	2
Don't know	8
Refused	9

What best describes his/her race-ethnicity?

American Indian or Alaska Native	1
Asian	2
Black or African American	3
Hispanic or Latino	4
Native Hawaiian or other Pacific Islander	5
White	6
Don't know	8
Refused	9

Is he/she currently an owner of the company?

Yes	1
No	2
Don't know	8
Refused	9

Was he/she an owner of the company before it became public?

Yes	1
No	2
Don't know	8
Refused	9

OK, for [Founder 2], that is a man (woman) correct?

Male	1
Female	2
Don't know	8
Refused	9

Can you tell me if he/she was born in the U.S. or somewhere else?

[DEFINITION: U.S. includes Puerto Rico, Guam, etc. and territories]

U.S.	1
Somewhere else	2
Don't know	8
Refused	9

What country was that?
About how many years has he/she lived in the U.S.?
[If deceased: About how many years was he/she in the U.S. when he/she passed away?] Is he/she now a U.S. citizen?

Yes	1
No	2
Don't know	8
Refused	9

What is his/her highest level of education? Would you say high school or less, some college, two-year college or technical degree, four-year college degree, Master's degree or doctoral/professional degree?

High school degree or less	1
Some college	2
Two year college or technical degree	3
Four year college degree	4
Master's degree	5
Doctoral/professional degree	6
Don't know	8
Refused	9

Was the most recent education obtained in the U.S.?

Yes	1
No	2
Don't know	8
Refused	9

What best describes his/her race-ethnicity?

American Indian or Alaska Native	1
Asian	2
Black or African American	3
Hispanic or Latino	4
Native Hawaiian or other Pacific Islander	5
White	6
Don't know	8
Refused	9

Is he/she currently an owner of the company?

Yes	1
No	2
Don't know	8
Refused	9

Was he/she an owner of the company before it became public?

Yes	1
No	2
Don't know	8
Refused	9

OK, for [Founder 3], that is a man (woman) correct?

Male	1
Female	2
Don't know	8
Refused	9

Can you tell me if he/she was born in the U.S. or somewhere else? [DEFINITION: U.S. includes Puerto Rico, Guam, etc. and territories]

U.S.	1
Somewhere else	2
Don't know	8
Refused	9

What country was that?
About how many years has he/she lived in the U.S.?
[If deceased: About how many years was he/she in the U.S. when he/she passed away?]
Is he/she now a U.S. citizen?

Yes	1
No	2
Don't know	8
Refused	9

What is his/her highest level of education? Would you say high school or less, some college, two-year college or technical degree, four-year college degree, Master's degree or doctoral/professional degree?

High school degree or less	1
Some college	2
Two year college or technical degree	3
Four year college degree	4
Master's degree	5
Doctoral/professional degree	6
Don't know	8
Refused	9

Was the most recent education obtained in the U.S.?

Yes	1
No	2
Don't know	8
Refused	9

What best describes his/her race-ethnicity?

American Indian or Alaska Native	1
Asian	2
Black or African American	3
Hispanic or Latino	4
Native Hawaiian or other Pacific Islander	5
White	6
Don't know	8
Refused	9

Is he/she currently an owner of the company?

Yes	1
No	2
Don't know	8
Refused	9

Was he/she an owner of the company before it became public?

Yes	1
No	2
Don't know	8
Refused	9

OK, for [Founder 4], that is a man (woman) correct?

Male	1
Female	2
Don't know	8
Refused	9

Can you tell me if he/she was born in the U.S. or somewhere else? [DEFINITION: U.S. includes Puerto Rico, Guam, etc. and territories]

U.S.	1
Somewhere else	2
Don't know	8
Refused	9

What is his/her highest level of education? Would you say high school or less, some college, two-year college or technical degree, four-year college degree, Master's degree or doctoral/professional degree?

High school degree or less	1
Some college	2
Two year college or technical degree	3
Four year college degree	4
Master's degree	5
Doctoral/professional degree	6
Don't know	8
Refused	9

What country was that?
About how many years has he/she lived in the U.S.?
[If deceased: About how many years was he/she in the U.S. when he/she passed away?]
Is he/she now a U.S. citizen?

Yes	1
No	2
Don't know	8
Refused	9

Was the most recent education obtained in the U.S.?

Yes	1
No	2
Don't know	8
Refused	9

What best describes his/her race-ethnicity?

American Indian or Alaska Native	1
Asian	2
Black or African American	3
Hispanic or Latino	4
Native Hawaiian or other Pacific Islander	5
White	6
Don't know	8
Refused	9

Is he/she currently an owner of the company?

Yes	1
No	2
Don't know	8
Refused	9

Was he/she an owner of the company before it became public?

Yes	1
No	2
Don't know	8
Refused	9

OK, for [Founder 5], that is a man (woman) correct?

Male	1
Female	2
Don't know	8
Refused	9

Can you tell me if he/she was born in the U.S. or somewhere else? [DEFINITION: U.S. includes Puerto Rico, Guam, etc. and territories]

U.S.	1
Somewhere else	2
Don't know	8
Refused	9

What country was that?

About how many years has he/she lived in the U.S.?

[If deceased: About how many years was he/she in the U.S. when he/she passed away?]

Is he/she now a U.S. citizen?

Yes	1
No	2
Don't know	8
Refused	9

What is his/her highest level of education? Would you say high school or less, some college, two-year college or technical degree, four-year college degree, Master's degree or doctoral/professional degree?

High school degree or less	1
Some college	2
Two year college or technical degree	3
Four year college degree	4
Master's degree	5
Doctoral/professional degree	6
Don't know	8
Refused	9

Was the most recent education obtained in the U.S.?

Yes	1
No	2
Don't know	8
Refused	9

What best describes his/her race-ethnicity?

American Indian or Alaska Native	1
Asian	2
Black or African American	3
Hispanic or Latino	4
Native Hawaiian or other Pacific Islander	5
White	6
Don't know	8
Refused	9

What one or more of the following things would you say brought the founders together to start this business?

Family	1
Attended school/college together	2
Worked together previously	3
Got together to start this business	4
Something else	5
More than one reason	6
Don't know	8
Refused	9

Is he/she currently an owner of the company?

Yes	1
No	2
Don't know	8
Refused	9

Was he/she an owner of the company before it became public?

Yes	1
No	2
Don't know	8
Refused	9

[Other reason] What was it?

Thank you very much for helping out with this study. If you have any questions you can contact _____ by email at_____.

End Notes

[1] As we describe in more detail below, a high-impact company is a firm with sales that have at least doubled over the most recent 4-year period and which has an employment growth quantifier of 2 or greater over the same period. High-tech is defined by the 3-digit SIC codes listed in Appendix A.

[2] We use the term "immigrants" in place of "foreign-born" here and in similar spots in this text because, as we note in the text and show in detail later, the vast majority of foreign-born high-tech entrepreneurs in the United States have been in this country for decades and have become citizens. However, we would acknowledge that "foreign-born" would be a more precise term in certain contexts.

[3] Most research shows that the use of state incentives to induce external investment in branch plants (so-called "smokestack chasing") has "little or no impact" (Peters and Fisher 2004, 32). By "organic growth," we mean growth without such subsidized investment.

[4] The Obama administration has suggested that it will seek comprehensive immigration reform legislation in the current Congress.

[5] USCIS reported on April 9, 2009, that it had received approximately 42,000 H-1B visa applications for the fiscal 2010 year, which begins in October.

[6] Portes, Guarnizo, and Haller (2002, 279) define transnationalism in this fashion: "In recent years, a new concept, "transnationalism," has introduced an alternative analytic stance in international migration studies. Instead of focusing on traditional concerns about origins of immigrants and their adaptation to receiving societies, this emerging perspective concentrates on the continuing relations between immigrants and their places of origin and how this back-and-forth traffic builds complex social fields that straddle national borders."

[7] The Kauffman Firm Survey uses the term "medium-tech" as well as "high-tech." Our definition of "hightech," described below, encompasses both of these categories, so we will use that term here.

[8] The employment growth quantifier (EGQ) is the product of the absolute and percent change in employment over a 4-year period of time, expressed as a decimal. EGQ is used to mitigate the unfavorable impact of measuring employment change solely in either percent or absolute terms, since the former favors small companies and the latter large businesses.

[9] In order to maintain historical continuity, the ACSL uses SIC codes rather than NAICS codes.

[10] We dropped SIC 874, management and public relations, which met the BLS definition. Nearly 15,000 HICs were found in this SIC, a very large number, which would have skewed our results.

[11] We did not ask the race of foreign-born founders, because of the great variation in racial and ethnic definitions and identities across the many countries of origin of these founders.

[12] In Canada and Australia, provinces and states play an active role in immigration policy.

In: Immigrant Entrepreneurship in the U.S. ISBN: 978-1-60876-816-5
Editor: Christian D. Knowles © 2010 Nova Science Publishers, Inc.

Chapter 2

ESTIMATING THE CONTRIBUTION OF IMMIGRANT BUSINESS OWNERS TO THE U.S. ECONOMY[*]

Robert W. Fairlie

EXECUTIVE SUMMARY

A better understanding of how immigrants contribute to the U.S. economy is important. Few studies have examined how immigrant entrepreneurs contribute to total U.S. business ownership, formation, and income. Using data from three large, nationally representative government datasets—the 2000 Census 5 percent Public Use Microdata (PUMS) Sample, the 1996-2007 Current Population Survey (CPS), and the 1992 Characteristics of Business Owners (CBO)—this study examines the contributions of immigrant business owners and their businesses to the U.S. economy.

To provide a comprehensive picture of the contributions of immigrant business owners, several measures are examined. First, the total number of immigrant business owners based on household survey data is estimated from the 2000 Census. Second, the number of new immigrant business owners per month is estimated from newly created data matching consecutive months of

---

[*] This is an edited, reformatted and augmented version of a Small Business Administration publication dated November 2008.

the 1996-2007 CPS. Third, total immigrant-owned business income is estimated from the 2000 Census. Finally, the total sales and employment of immigrant-owned businesses based on business tax records are estimated from the 1992 CBO. The following are among the key findings:

1. The nearly 1.5 million immigrant business owners in the United States represent 12.5 percent of all business owners. Immigrants constitute 12.2 percent of the total work force in the United States. They own a large share of businesses in the lowest- and highest-skill sectors and in several industries, an indication that their contributions differ across sectors of the economy. Immigrant business ownership is geographically concentrated in a few states. Nearly 30 percent of all business owners in California are immigrants. One-fourth of New York business owners are foreign-born, as are more than one-fifth of business owners in New Jersey, Florida, and Hawaii.
2. Immigrants are nearly 30 percent more likely to start a business than nonimmigrants, and they represent 16.7 percent of all new business owners in the United States. In California, immigrants constitute 34.2 percent of all new business owners each month and they represent roughly 5 percent of all new business owners in the United States. Nearly 30 percent of all new business owners per month in New York, Florida, and Texas, are immigrants.
3. The total business income generated by immigrant business owners is $67 billion, 11.6 percent of all business income in the United States. Immigrant business owners generate nearly $20 billion or one-quarter of all business income in California, and nearly one-fifth of all business income in New York, Florida, and New Jersey.
4. Immigrants own 11.2 percent of all businesses with $100,000 or more in sales and 10.8 percent of all businesses with employees.
5. Although business owners from Mexico constitute the largest share of immigrant business owners, immigrants from around the world are sources of U.S. business formation, ownership, and income.

These findings indicate that immigrants make large and important contributions to business ownership, formation, and income in the United States, particularly in some states and economic sectors.

INTRODUCTION

The entrepreneurial success of immigrants is well known. For example, business ownership is higher among the foreign-born than the native-born in many developed countries including the United States, the United Kingdom, Canada, and Australia (Borjas, 1986, Schuetze and Antecol, 2006, and Fairlie et al., 2008). Businesses owned by some immigrant groups are also very successful, with higher incomes and employment than native-owned businesses. Many developed countries have created special visas and entry requirements in an attempt to attract immigrant entrepreneurs (Schuetze and Antecol, 2006). The United States has a small program that gives special preferences for admission to immigrants who invest $1 million in businesses that create at least 10 new full-time jobs (U.S. Department of Homeland Security, 2007).

Recently, much attention has been drawn to the contributions of immigrant entrepreneurs to the technology and engineering sectors of the economy. Twenty-five percent of engineering and technology companies started in the past decade were founded by immigrants (Wadwha, et al., 2007). These firms had $52 billion in sales and hired 450,000 workers in 2005 in the United States. Previous research also indicates that immigrant entrepreneurs have made important contributions to high-tech areas such as Silicon Valley (Saxenian, 1999, 2000). Engineers from China and India run roughly one-quarter of all technology businesses started in Silicon Valley. These firms have created substantial wealth and many high-tech jobs in the area. High rates of immigrant entrepreneurship also contribute to overall business creation in Silicon Valley (Fairlie, 2007).

Although many previous studies examine immigrant business ownership, very little is known about business formation rates and business performance among immigrants. Previous research examining the contributions of immigrant business owners has generally focused on specific sectors of the economy or regions of the country. A broader understanding of immigrant business ownership at the national level and for all sectors is needed. The lack of data availability on immigrant-owned businesses has been a major hindrance for research in this area. Limited evidence is available on how many new businesses are created by immigrants, the types of businesses created by these immigrants, and the countries of origin for these immigrant business owners. Thus, the contribution of immigrant-owned businesses to the total U.S. economy is not well understood.

In this study, the contribution of immigrants to business ownership, formation, and performance is examined using three large nationally representative datasets—the Census 5 percent PUMS sample, the Current Population Survey (CPS), and the Characteristics of Business Owners (CBO). The Census 5 percent PUMS sample is the only nationally representative dataset with large enough sample sizes to examine business ownership among detailed immigrant groups, and the CBO is the only business-level dataset with information on a large sample of immigrants. Consecutive months of CPS data are matched to address the absence of longitudinal data with large immigrant samples to study business formation.[1] The matched CPS data allow for a detailed analysis of rates of business creation among the foreign-born.

The goal of this study is to provide a comprehensive analysis of immigrant business ownership and immigrants' contributions to the U.S. economy. Several key questions about immigrant business ownership are explored using Census, CPS, and CBO data:

- How much do immigrant groups contribute to total business ownership in the United States?
- Do immigrants have higher business ownership rates than nonimmigrants and what percent of all businesses do immigrants own?
- Where do immigrant business owners come from and do immigrant-owned businesses contribute more to specific sectors of the U.S. economy?
- How do immigrants contribute to new business starts?
- Are business formation rates higher among immigrants and do immigrants start a disproportionate share of businesses requiring certain skill levels or in certain industries and states?
- What is the contribution of immigrant-owned businesses to total business income, sales, and employment in the United States?
- In which industries and parts of the country do immigrants generate large shares of total U.S. business income?

DATA

The only nationally representative and publicly available datasets with large enough samples to study immigrant business owners in detail are the

Census 5 percent PUMS sample and the Current Population Survey. Although both are cross-sectional datasets, consecutive months of the CPS can be matched creating monthly panel data following Fairlie (2008).[2] This is important for the creation of a measure of the rate of business formation at the individual owner level. Cross-sectional datasets allow only for the calculation of the total number of existing business owners. The combination of 2000 Census microdata and matched CPS data allows for a detailed study of immigrant business ownership and formation in the United States. Published estimates from the Characteristics of Business Owners provide further evidence on the contributions of immigrant-owned businesses. Each dataset is described in turn.

The 2000 Census

The primary sample used to examine immigrant business ownership and net business income is the 5 percent Public Use Microdata Sample (PUMS) of the 2000 U.S. Census of Population. The Census microdata include over 8 million observations for working-age adults. Even after conditioning on business ownership, the sample size is very large, allowing one to explore the causes of differences in net business incomes. The Census is also large enough to examine regional, industrial, and country-of-origin differences across immigrant business owners.

Using the Census data, business ownership is measured based on the class-ofworker question that refers to the respondent's main job or business activity (i.e., activity with the most hours) at the time of the interview. Business owners are individuals who report that they are 1) "self-employed in own not incorporated business, professional practice, or farm," or 2) "self-employed in own incorporated business, professional practice, or farm." This definition includes owners of all types of businesses—incorporated, unincorporated, employer, and nonemployer firms. The samples used in this analysis include all business owners of ages 20 and over who work 15 or more hours per week in their businesses. To rule out very small-scale businesses, disguised unemployment, or casual sellers of goods and services, only business owners with 15 or more hours worked are included.[3] Fifteen hours per week is chosen as the cutoff because it represents a reasonable amount of work effort in the business, about two days per week. Note that self-employed business ownership is defined as the individual's main job activity, thus removing the potential for counting side businesses owned by wage-andsalary workers.

Matched Current Population Survey, 1996-2007

Although research on entrepreneurship is growing rapidly, very few national datasets provide information on recent trends in business formation. A relatively new measure to study immigrant-owned business formation is matched data from the 1996-2007 Current Population Surveys (CPS). The new measure captures the rate of business creation at the individual owner level. The underlying datasets used to create the entrepreneurship or business formation measure are the basic monthly files of the Current Population Survey (CPS). Longitudinal data can be created by linking the CPS files over time. The surveys, conducted monthly by the U.S. Bureau of the Census and the U.S. Bureau of Labor Statistics, are representative of the entire U.S. population and contain observations for more than 130,000 people. Combining the 1996 to 2007 monthly data creates a sample size of more than 8 million adult observations.

Households in the CPS are interviewed each month over a four-month period. Eight months later they are re-interviewed in each month of a second four-month period. Thus, individuals who are interviewed in January, February, March, and April of one year are interviewed again in January, February, March, and April of the following year. The rotation pattern of the CPS thus allows for matching information on individuals monthly for 75 percent of all respondents to each survey. To match these data, the author uses the household and individual identifiers provided by the CPS and removes false matches by comparing race, sex, and age codes from the two months. All nonunique matches are also removed from the dataset. Monthly match rates are generally between 94 and 96 percent, and false positive rates are very low.

Potential measures of the number of existing business owners or businesses are readily available from several nationally representative government datasets. For example, the Economic Census's Survey of Business Owners provides estimates of the total number of businesses every five years, and the CPS provides estimates of the total number of self-employed business owners every month.[4] Typical measures of business ownership based on these data, however, do not capture the dynamic nature of business creation. In particular, they do not measure business formation at the time the business is created.[5]

The business formation rate is estimated by first identifying all individuals who do not own a business as their main job in the first survey month, then matching CPS files to determine whether they own a business as their main job (with 15 or more usual hours worked per week) in the following survey month. The business formation rate is thus defined as the percentage of the population of non-business owners who start a business each month. To identify whether they are business owners in each month, the author uses information on their main job, defined as the one with the most hours worked. Thus, individuals who start side or casual businesses are not counted if they are working more hours on a wage-and-salary job.[6]

Characteristics of Business Owners, 1992

Estimates of business ownership and formation rates and of the net business income of owners are available using Census and CPS microdata, but another approach to examining the question is to use business-level data, where the business, rather than the owner, is the focus of the analysis. The main advantage of these data is that they typically provide more information on business performance than individual-level data, but the main disadvantage is that they do not include information on the demographic characteristics of the owner. (See Headd and Saade, 2008, and Fairlie and Robb, 2008, for more discussion on the comparison between individual-level and business-level data on entrepreneurship.) Unfortunately, the only large nationally representative business- level data in which the immigrant status of the owner is known are in the 1992 Characteristics of Business Owners (CBO).[7] The most recent version of the CBO, the 2002 Survey of Business Owners (SBO), does not include information on the immigrant status of the owner. Because the CBO microdata are confidential and access is restricted, the only estimates presented are U.S. Census Bureau figures for 1997.

COMPARISON OF MEASURES OF BUSINESS OWNERSHIP AND IMMIGRATION

Before estimating the contribution of immigrants to U.S. business ownership, formation and income, it is useful to briefly compare measures of business ownership. A brief discussion of the issues will illuminate the following analysis, which uses several different measures and datasets. Table 1 reports estimates of the number of business owners, businesses and new business owners from the most commonly used government sources that include at least limited information on the owner (see Fairlie and Robb, 2008, for more discussion of data sources).

Table 1. Comparison of Estimates of Number of U.S. Business Owners and Businesses

	Immigrants	U.S. total
Total number of self-employed business owners (Census 2000)	1,436,410	11,521,910
Total number of businesses (Survey of Business Owners 2002)	Not available	22,480,256
Total number of businesses (Characteristics of Business Owners 1992)	1,617,482	17,253,143
Total number of new business owners per month (Matched Current Population Survey 1996-2007)	81,100	484,864
Total number of employer firm births (Statistics of U.S. Businesses 2004-2005)	Not available	644,122
Total legal permanent residents, naturalizations and refugees (U.S. Department of Homeland Security 2007)	1,761,109	Not applicable
Total work force (Census 2000)	14,781,400	121,440,670

Notes: 1) The total number of self-employed business owners from the 2000 Census includes business owners with 15 or more hours worked per usual week. 2) The total number of businesses from the 2002 SBO is based on tax records and excludes publicly held, foreign-owned, not-forprofit, and other firms. 3) The total number of businesses from the 1992 CBO is based on tax records and does not include C corporations. 4) The total number of new business owners per month from the matched CPS 1996-2007 includes new business owners with 15 or more hours worked per week. 5) The total number of employer firm births from the SUSB includes only new employer firms. 6) The total work force from the 2000 Census includes all workers with 15 or more hours worked per usual week. Sources: Author's calculations based on 2000 Census microdata and 1996-2007 Matched CPS microdata, U.S. Census Bureau (1997), U.S. Census Bureau (2006), U.S. Department of Homeland Security (2007), Statistics of U.S. Businesses (2004-05), and Fairlie and Robb (2008).

Estimates from the 2000 Census data indicate that there are 11.5 million self-employed business owners in the United States. In comparison, estimates from the well known and commonly referenced 2002 Survey of Business Owners (SBO), also conducted by the U.S. Census Bureau, indicate that there are 22.5 million businesses in the United States.[8] Why do these estimates differ so much? First, the Census 2000 estimates of the number of business owners are based on household survey data and enumerate individual business owners. The SBO includes all business operations during 2002 that filed tax forms as individual proprietorships, partnerships, or any type of corporation. Second, the 2000 Census estimates include only individuals owning businesses as their main work activity with a substantial commitment of hours. The SBO includes all firms with receipts of $1,000 or more, which may include side or "casual" businesses owned by wage-and-salary workers, the unemployed, or retired workers. Roughly 30 percent of business owners in the SBO report working less than 20 hours per week in the business (U.S. Census Bureau, 2006). Third, the Census 2000 estimates include all business owners, whereas the SBO excludes agriculture and a few other types of businesses. Finally, Census 2000 estimates of the number of business owners and SBO estimates of the number of businesses differ because of multiple owners of businesses, individuals who own multiple businesses, workers in occupations such as sales and real estate, the reference period for capturing business ownership, and other measurement issues (see Headd, 2005, Headd and Saade, 2008, Bjelland et al., 2006, and Fairlie and Robb, 2008, for more discussion).

The 2002 SBO does not include information on the immigrant status of the owner. Estimates here of the number of immigrant-owned businesses are from the 1992 CBO. The 2000 Census indicates that there are 1.4 million immigrant business owners in the United States, and the 1992 CBO indicates that there are 1.6 million immigrant-owned businesses. Estimates of the number of immigrant and total business owners from the Census and estimates of the number of immigrant-owned and all businesses from the CBO differ for reasons similar to those noted above.[9] The main difference is that the CBO is based on tax records and thus includes small-scale business activities and other individuals who do not consider their main work activity to be self-employment.

Table 1 also reports estimates of the number of new business owners each month from the matched CPS 1996-2007 data. The CPS data indicate that there are 484,864 new business owners and 81,100 new immigrant business owners in the United States each month. A measure of business starts that has been commonly used in the previous literature is employer firm births from the

Statistics of U.S. Businesses (SUSB) created by the U.S. Census Bureau.[10] The SUSB data, however, capture a narrower range of entrepreneurial activity than estimates reported here from the matched CPS data. These data, collected by the U.S. Census Bureau and summarized by the U.S. Small Business Administration (SBA), Office of Advocacy, include only employer firms. The exclusion of nonemployer firms is likely to lead to a substantial undercount of the rate of business formation because nonemployer firms represent 75 percent of all firms (U.S. Small Business Administration, 2001, Headd, 2005) and a significant number of new employer firms start as nonemployer firms (Davis, et. al., 2006). Estimates of business formation from the CPS do not suffer from this problem because they include all new employer and nonemployer firms. Indeed, as reported in Table 1, the SUSB data indicate that there were 644,122 new employer firm births from 2004 to 2005 in the United States. It is also difficult to compare these estimates to the CPS estimates because they are based on business-level data, whereas the CPS is based on individual-level data. Furthermore, the matched CPS data provide estimates of the number of new business owners per month, which allows for individuals to start and stop multiple businesses over the year. Thus, an annual estimate of the number of new business owners from the CPS data cannot simply be obtained by multiplying these estimates by 12.

Table 1 also reports estimates of the total number of immigrants in the United States. Estimates from the U.S. Department of Homeland Security (2007) indicate that there were 1.8 million new legal permanent residents, naturalizations, and refugees/aslyees in 2007. These estimates capture the flow of immigrants, but it is more useful to estimate the number of immigrants currently residing in the United States (the stock of immigrants) to identify the total contributions of immigrant business owners. Estimates from the 2000 Census indicate that there are 14.8 million immigrants in the U.S. work force. Immigrants represent 12.2 percent of the total work force in the United States.

BUSINESS OWNERSHIP

Using microdata from the Census and matched CPS, business ownership rates, business formation rates, and business performance among immigrants are examined. What is the contribution of immigrants to the stock of business owners in the United States? What is the immigrant contribution to the number of new business owners? How much total business income do businesses owned by the foreign-born generate? Focusing on business formation separate from business performance is important for providing a comprehensive view of the state of immigrant business ownership. Demographic disparities in business formation and business longevity are the underlying causes of differences in business ownership.

Examining the contribution of immigrants to the economy entails estimating the total number of immigrant business owners in the United States and comparing that to the total number of business owners. Table 2 reports estimates of the total number of immigrant business owners from the 2000 Census. The 2000 Census is the latest available dataset with large enough samples to examine detailed immigrant groups. Estimates from the 2000 Census indicate that there are nearly 1.5 million immigrant business owners, representing 12.5 percent of all 11.5 million business owners in the United States.

The immigrant share of all business owners compares favorably to the immigrant share of the work force. Immigrants constitute 12.2 percent of the total U.S. work force, implying a higher business ownership rate than the U.S.-born rate. Indeed, 9.7 percent of immigrants own a business, compared with 9.5 percent of the U.S.-born work force. This finding is consistent with the previous literature that documents higher business ownership rates among immigrants (see Schuetze and Antecol, 2006 for example). The difference in business ownership rates, however, is not large.

Is the higher rate of business ownership among immigrants attributable to favorable characteristics, such as education, age, marital status, region, and other demographic characteristics? This question is investigated by estimating multivariate regressions that control for detailed demographic characteristics of the work force. Regression models allow one to identify the independent effect of different factors on business ownership. The detailed demographic information available in the Census microdata makes it possible to control for many important determinants of business ownership.

Specification 1 of Table 3 reports marginal effects estimates from a probit regression for the probability of business ownership using the 2000 Census.[11] A probit model is commonly used to estimate regression models in which the dependent variable takes on only the values of 0 and 1. With this model, the probability of being a business owner is expressed as:

$$\text{Prob}(Y=1) = \Phi(\alpha + X\beta + I\gamma).$$

Table 2. Number of Business Owners by Immigrant Group, Census 2000

Group	Business owners		Total work force		Business ownership rate (percent)
	Number	Percent of U.S. total	Number	Percent of U.S. total	
U.S. total	11,521,910	100.00	121,440,670	100.00	9.5
U.S.-born total	10,085,500	87.53	106,659,270	87.83	9.5
Immigrant total	1,436,410	12.47	14,781,400	12.17	9.7
Mexico	255,300	2.22	3,944,740	3.25	6.5
Korea	90,280	0.78	400,110	0.33	22.6
India	60,210	0.52	596,010	0.49	10.1
China	57,590	0.50	610,540	0.50	9.4
Vietnam	51,720	0.45	523,460	0.43	9.9
Canada	50,400	0.44	388,480	0.32	13.0
Cuba	49,090	0.43	379,650	0.31	12.9
Germany	41,430	0.36	315,710	0.26	13.1
Philippines	36,860	0.32	785,170	0.65	4.7
Italy	34,520	0.30	190,700	0.16	18.1
Iran	33,570	0.29	156,310	0.13	21.5
El Salvador	31,180	0.27	411,450	0.34	7.6
Poland	30,810	0.27	226,730	0.19	13.6
England	27,530	0.24	222,730	0.18	12.4
Colombia	25,760	0.22	243,560	0.20	10.6
Taiwan	23,480	0.20	176,840	0.15	13.3
Greece	20,730	0.18	79,750	0.07	26.0
Dominican Republic	19,960	0.17	271,450	0.22	7.4
Jamaica	18,980	0.16	316,070	0.26	6.0
Guatemala	18,710	0.16	231,500	0.19	8.1

Notes: 1) The sample consists of all workers with 15 or more hours worked per usual week. The total sample size is 5,967,675. 2) All reported estimates use sample weights provided by the 2000 Census. 3) The reported immigrant groups represent the largest 20 groups based on the number of business owners. Source: Author's calculations from 2000 Census microdata.

Table 3. Probit and Linear Regressions for Business Ownership, Formation and Income Census (2000) and Matched Current Population Survey (1996-2007)

Explanatory variables Dependent variable	(1) Business ownership	(2) Business formation	(3) Log business income
Data source	2000 Census	CPS	2000 Census
Immigrant	0.0180	0.0009	0.0201
	(0.0005)	(0.0001)	(0.0069)
Black	-0.0677	-0.0012	-0.1651
	(0.0005)	(0.0001)	(0.0090)
Latino	-0.0464	-0.0004	-0.1380
	(0.0005)	(0.0001)	(0.0086)
Asian	-0.0267	-0.0013	-0.0360
	(0.0007)	(0.0001)	(0.0109)
Native American	-0.0324	-0.0005	-0.3209
	(0.0015)	(0.0002)	(0.0251)
Female	-0.0495	-0.0021	-0.7106
	(0.0002)	(0.0000)	(0.0039)
Age	0.0054	0.0003	0.0925
	(0.0001)	(0.0000)	(0.0009)
Age squared	0.0000	0.0000	-0.0010
	(0.0000)	(0.0000)	(0.0000)
High school graduate	-0.0049	0.0003	0.1620
	(0.0004)	(0.0001)	(0.0064)
Some college	-0.0053	0.0006	0.3052
	(0.0004)	(0.0001)	(0.0064)
College graduate	0.0019	0.0011	0.8501
	(0.0004)	(0.0001)	(0.0063)
Mean of dependent variable	0.0949	0.0028	10.0569
Sample size	5,967,675	7,789,698	596,385

Notes: 1) The sample includes all workers with 15 or more hours worked per usual week in Specification 1, all non-business owners in the first survey month in Specification 2, and all business owners with 15 or more hours worked per usual week in Specification 3. 2) The probability of business ownership is estimated using a probit model in Specification 1, the probability of starting a business is estimated using a probit model in Specification 2, and log business income is estimated using a linear regression in Specification 3. 3) Marginal effects and their standard errors are reported for Specifications 1 and 2. 4) Although not reported, Specifications 1 and 3 also include marital status, children and region as independent variables, and Specification 2 also includes martial status, region, urbanicity, and year of survey as independent variables.

where Y=1 if the individual is a business owner and Y=0 if the individual is a wage/salary worker, b is the normal distribution, α is a constant term, X includes the demographic variables such as education, age and region, and I is a dummy variable equal to 1 if the individual is an immigrant. In this model, γ provides an estimate of the difference between immigrants and the native-born in the business ownership rate after controlling for the effects of education, age, and other individual characteristics. The probit regressions include immigrant status and controls for broad racial/ethnic categories, gender, age, marital status, children, and region.

The probit estimates indicate that African Americans, Latinos, Asians, and Native Americans are less likely to own businesses after controlling for other factors. Women are found to be much less likely to own businesses than are men. As in previous research, education is positively related to education and business ownership (see van der Sluis, van Praag and Vijverberg, 2004, and Moutray, 2007, for recent reviews of the literature). The relationship between business ownership and age is generally positive. Overall, these findings from 2000 Census microdata are consistent with findings from the previous literature on the determinants of business ownership (see Parker, 2004, and Fairlie and Robb, 2008, for recent reviews of the literature on the determinants of business ownership).

The key coefficient of interest in this analysis is immigrant status. After controlling for racial, gender, education, family, and regional differences, the author finds that immigrants are more likely than nonimmigrants to own businesses. The marginal effect estimate is 0.018, implying that immigrants are 1.8 percentage points more likely to own a business than are the U.S.-born. This is larger than the raw difference of 0.3 percentage points in business ownership rates reported in Table 1, suggesting that immigrants would have even higher business ownership rates in the United States if they had characteristics more similar to those of the U.S.-born.

Source Countries

What are the main source countries of immigrant business owners in the United States? In addition to the immigrant total contribution, Table 2 also reports estimates of the number of business owners by source country for the top 20 countries. The largest contributing country is Mexico, with 255,300 business owners representing 2.22 percent of all business owners in the United

States. Korean immigrant business owners make up the next largest share of business owners, with 0.78 percent or 90,280. Indian, Chinese, Vietnamese, Canadian, and Cuban immigrants also represent relatively large shares of immigrant business owners in the United States. Of these groups, Mexican immigrants have a rate of business ownership substantially below the national average (6.5 percent compared with 9.5 percent). The large contribution to the total number of immigrant business owners is thus being driven by the large share of Mexican immigrants in the United States and not by higher business ownership rates. In contrast, 22.6 percent of Korean immigrants own a business, one reason they represent the second largest number of immigrant business owners in the United States.

Overall, immigrants contribute substantially to the number of business owners in the United States. These businesses are also quite diverse; Mexican immigrants are the only group representing more than 10 percent of the total immigrant share of business owners. Business owners in the United States come from countries around the world.

Education, Industry and State Contributions

Immigrant business owners constitute a large share of all business owners in the United States. What is their contribution to different parts of the U.S. economy? Immigrant business owners contribute differently to high-skilled businesses, industries, and states. Education is used as a proxy for skill level based on available Census data. Table 4 reports estimates of the number of immigrant business owners by education level. Immigrant business owners make up the largest share of the least educated business owners. Slightly more than 28 percent of all business owners with less than a high school degree are immigrants. This educational group represents 27.2 percent of all immigrant business owners in the United States. The largest educational group among immigrants is college graduates, who constitute 31.3 percent of all immigrant business owners, and immigrant business owners represent 11.9 percent of all business owners with a college education. Interestingly, immigrant business owners contribute much less to the middle of the educational distribution—those who have completed high school but not college. This is because immigrants represent a smaller share of the U.S. population for these education levels.

Table 4. Number of Immigrant Business Owners by Education Level Census 2000

Industry	Immigrant business owners			All business owners	
	Number	Percent of immigrant total	Percent of U.S. education total	Number	Percent of U.S. total
All education levels	1,436,420	100.0	12.5	11,521,920	100.0
Less than high school	390,690	27.2	28.4	1,376,540	11.9
High school graduate	285,710	19.9	9.6	2,977,700	25.8
Some college	310,100	21.6	9.1	3,399,700	29.5
College graduate	449,920	31.3	11.9	3,767,980	32.7

Notes: 1) The sample includes all business owners with 15 or more hours worked per usual week. 2) All reported estimates use sample weights provided by the 2000 Census. Source: Author's calculations from 2000 Census microdata.

Similar to the analysis by skill level, it is useful to examine how immigrant- owned businesses contribute to specific industries in the United States (Table 5). Immigrant business owners make notable contributions to the U.S. economy in several industries. More than one-fifth of all businesses in the arts, entertainment and recreation industry are owned by immigrants. This is nearly double the 12.5 percent immigrant contribution to all industries. Immigrant-owned businesses also contribute substantially to other services (17.6 percent), transportation (16.9 percent), wholesale trade (15.9 percent), and retail trade (15.5 percent).

Immigrants are heavily concentrated in California, New York, Florida, and Texas (U.S. Department of Homeland Security, 2007) and may contribute more to the economies of these states than others. Table 6 reports estimates of the number of immigrant business owners by state and Figure 1 displays estimates for the top 10 states. California has by far the largest number of immigrant business owners, with 427,580. These immigrant business owners represent a very large share of all business owners in the state. Nearly 30 percent of all business owners in California are immigrants. Roughly one-fourth of all business owners in New York one one-fifth in New Jersey,

Florida, and Hawaii are foreign-born. Immigrant contributions to business ownership in all these states are substantially higher than the national average of 12.5 percent.

Table 5. Number of Immigrant Business Owners by Industry Census 2000

Industry	Immigrant business owners			All business owners	
	Number	Percent of immigrant total	Percent of U.S. industry total	Number	Percent of U.S. total
All industries	1,436,410	100.0	12.5	11,521,910	100.0
Agriculture and mining	26,740	1.9	3.7	730,800	6.3
Construction	187,030	13.0	9.6	1,945,910	16.9
Manufacturing	73,070	5.1	13.6	535,550	4.6
Wholesale trade	60,900	4.2	15.9	383,370	3.3
Retail trade	182,850	12.7	15.5	1,176,230	10.2
Transportation	71,470	5.0	16.9	423,320	3.7
Information	16,330	1.1	9.2	177,290	1.5
Finance, insurance and real estate	76,900	5.4	8.6	889,800	7.7
Professional services	219,830	15.3	10.4	2,115,610	18.4
Education, health and social services	157,740	11.0	13.0	1,213,620	10.5
Arts, entertainment and recreation	144,240	10.0	21.1	683,390	5.9
Other services	219,320	15.3	17.6	1,247,020	10.8

Notes: 1) The sample includes all business owners with 15 or more hours worked per usual week. 2) All reported estimates use sample weights provided by the 2000 Census. Source: Author's calculations from 2000 Census microdata.

Table 6. Number of Immigrant Business Owners by State Census 2000

Industry	Immigrant business owners			All business owners	
	Number	Percent of immigrant total	Percent of state total	Number	Percent of U.S. total
U.S. total	1,436,410	100.0	12.5	11,521,910	100.0
Alabama	4,361	0.3	2.7	159,460	1.4
Alaska	1,946	0.1	7.5	25,990	0.2
Arizona	24,357	1.7	12.1	200,900	1.7
Arkansas	2,327	0.2	1.9	122,150	1.1
California	427,580	29.8	28.7	1,490,590	12.9
Colorado	15,875	1.1	6.6	241,150	2.1
Connecticut	19,741	1.4	13.2	149,810	1.3
Delaware	2,044	0.1	7.2	28,330	0.2
District of Columbia	2,787	0.2	16.2	17,230	0.1
Florida	146,039	10.2	20.6	710,530	6.2
Georgia	25,883	1.8	7.7	334,140	2.9
Hawaii	10,780	0.8	20.7	51,970	0.5
Idaho	2,390	0.2	3.4	70,280	0.6
Illinois	65,178	4.5	14.5	448,600	3.9
Indiana	7,351	0.5	3.3	219,980	1.9
Iowa	2,448	0.2	1.7	147,780	1.3
Kansas	4,305	0.3	3.4	128,360	1.1
Kentucky	3,331	0.2	2.1	154,960	1.3
Louisiana	7,940	0.6	5.0	159,200	1.4
Maine	2,421	0.2	3.3	74,180	0.6
Maryland	29,500	2.1	14.6	201,920	1.8
Massachusetts	33,372	2.3	12.6	265,850	2.3
Michigan	22,714	1.6	6.4	356,250	3.1
Minnesota	6,640	0.5	2.8	241,440	2.1
Mississippi	2,310	0.2	2.3	99,430	0.9
Missouri	7,151	0.5	3.0	236,350	2.1
Montana	950	0.1	1.5	64,600	0.6
Nebraska	1,356	0.1	1.4	97,270	0.8
Nevada	8,265	0.6	13.1	62,920	0.5

Table 6. (Continued)

Industry	Immigrant business owners			All business owners	
	Number	Percent of immigrant total	Percent of state total	Number	Percent of U.S. total
New Hampshire	3,442	0.2	5.5	63,010	0.5
New Jersey	68,870	4.8	21.4	321,310	2.8
New Mexico	6,816	0.5	8.6	79,700	0.7
New York	175,834	12.2	24.7	710,560	6.2
North Carolina	15,906	1.1	4.8	334,090	2.9
North Dakota	552	0.0	1.4	38,440	0.3
Ohio	16,341	1.1	4.1	395,450	3.4
Oklahoma	4,972	0.3	3.2	155,890	1.4
Oregon	13,786	1.0	7.4	187,050	1.6
Pennsylvania	26,519	1.8	6.1	435,390	3.8
Rhode Island	3,697	0.3	9.3	39,820	0.3
South Carolina	4,776	0.3	3.3	144,600	1.3
South Dakota	667	0.0	1.4	47,660	0.4
Tennessee	7,523	0.5	3.3	230,830	2.0
Texas	125,184	8.7	15.3	817,270	7.1
Utah	4,546	0.3	5.2	87,710	0.8
Vermont	1,479	0.1	3.6	41,170	0.4
Virginia	29,155	2.0	11.0	265,520	2.3
Washington	26,895	1.9	10.2	263,590	2.3
West Virginia	1,588	0.1	3.1	51,410	0.4
Wisconsin	5,907	0.4	2.7	222,320	1.9
Wyoming	615	0.0	2.2	27,500	0.2

Notes: 1) The sample consists of all business owners with 15 or more hours worked per usual week. 2) All reported estimates use sample weights provided by the 2000 Census. Source: Author's calculations from 2000 Census microdata.

BUSINESS FORMATION

The business ownership rate captures the stock of business owners in the economy at a given point in time, but does not capture the dynamics of business creation. In this section, the author examines business formation among immigrants. In particular, I estimate the number of new immigrant business owners and make comparisons to the total number of new business owners. This analysis captures how immigrants contribute to the flow of businesses in the U.S. economy. New businesses are often associated with economic growth, innovation, and the creation of jobs.

For the analysis of business formation, panel data are needed. The matched CPS (1996-2007) microdata, offering both panel data and very large sample sizes, constitute the only dataset in which business creation by immigrants can be examined. Table 7 reports estimates of the number of new immigrant business owners in the United States. Some 81,000 immigrants start businesses each month. This represents 16.7 percent of all new business owners in the United States, which is higher than the share of all business owners (stock) or of the work force. Indeed, immigrants are found to create businesses at a faster rate than nonimmigrants. The business formation rate per month among immigrants is 0.35 percent; that is, of 100,000 non-business-owning immigrants, 350 start a business each month. This rate of business formation is higher than the nonimmigrant rate of 0.27 percent, or 270 of 100,000 U.S.-born non-business owners per month. Although higher rates of business ownership have been documented extensively in the previous literature, the finding of substantially higher immigrant-owned business formation rates is a relatively new and important finding. Combined with the previous finding of slightly higher business ownership rates among immigrants relative to nonimmigrants, it indicates that immigrants move into and out of business ownership at much higher rates than nonimmigrants.[12]

Are these higher rates of business formation among immigrants attributable to differences in education and other demographic characteristics? Specification 2 of Table 3 reports estimates from probit regressions for the probability of starting a business each month using matched CPS data. Only non-business owners in the first survey month are included in the sample. The dependent variable equals 1 if the individual reports owning a business in the second survey month and 0 if they do not report owning a business in the second survey month. The estimates indicate that African Americans, Latinos, Asians, and Native Americans are less likely to start businesses after controlling for other factors. Women are also less likely to start businesses. Business creation generally increases with age and strongly increases with education. College graduates have a 0.11 percentage point higher rate of business creation per month than those with less than a high school education. This difference represents a monthly rate of 110 more new business owners per 100,000 people (or a rate 39 percent higher than the mean rate).

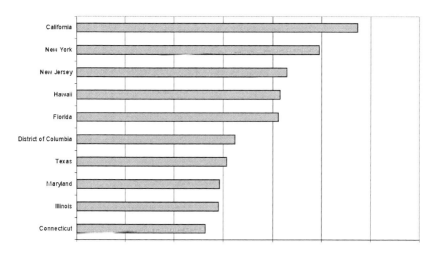

Figure 1. Immigrant Share of All Business Owners for Top 10 States Census 2000

The probit estimates indicate that immigrants are much more likely to start businesses after controlling for education and other factors. The coefficient estimates imply that immigrants are 0.09 percentage points more likely to start a business than the U.S.-born, or 90 more new business owners per 100,000 people. This rate of business creation is 32 percent higher than the mean rate. The regression-adjusted difference is slightly higher than the unadjusted difference of 70 per 100,000 as reported in Table 7. Business creation rates are much higher among immigrants and the difference is not a result of advantageous demographic characteristics.

Table 7 also reports estimates of the number of new business owners per month by source country.[13] The largest number of new businesses is created by immigrants from Mexico, who account for 4.8 percent of all business starts in the United States. Business formation is distributed across many other immigrant groups.

Education, Industry, and State Contributions

Immigrants may contribute differently to business creation in various sectors of the U.S. economy. For example, Wadwha et al. (2007) find that 25 percent of engineering and technology companies started in the past decade were founded by immigrants. Table 8 reports estimates of immigrant-owned business formation by education level. The largest contribution of new immigrant business owners by education level is from those who have lower than a high school education. These new immigrant business owners represent 35.8 percent of all new business owners in this skill group in the United States. Immigrants constitute 14.8 percent of all new business owners who are college graduates.

Among major industries, the highest representation of immigrant-owned business starts is in the wholesale and retail trade, and transportation and utilities industries. Table 9 reports estimates of the number of new immigrant business owners by industry. New immigrant business owners represent 23.1 percent of all new business owners in transportation and utilities and 22.7 percent of new business owners in wholesale and retail trade. Immigrants also constitute more than one-fifth of new business owners in the leisure and hospitality, and other services industries.

Table 7. Number of New Business Owners per Month by Immigrant Group Matched Current Population Survey (1996-2007)

Group	New business owners		Business formation rate	
	Number per month	Percent of U.S. total	Percent	Number per 100,000
U.S. total	484,864	100.00	0.28	284
U.S.-born total	403,763	83.27	0.27	273
Immigrant total	81,100	16.73	0.35	349
Mexico	23,094	4.76	0.34	340
El Salvador	3,178	0.66	0.47	472
Cuba	3,098	0.64	0.42	425
Korea	2,870	0.59	0.57	575
India	2,619	0.54	0.29	292
Dominican Republic	2,417	0.50	0.47	467
Guatemala	1,758	0.36	0.52	518
Jamaica	1,691	0.35	0.40	401
Vietnam	1,678	0.35	0.24	245
Canada	1,652	0.34	0.35	354

Notes: 1) The sample consists of non-business owners who do not own a business in the first survey month. The total sample size is 7,789,698. 2) Business formation is defined as those individuals who report starting a business in the second survey month with 15 or more hours worked per week. 3) The reported immigrant groups represent the largest 10 groups based on the number of new businesses. Source: Author's calculations from matched 1996-2007 CPS microdata.

Immigrants make very large contributions to business creation in several states (see Figure 2 and Table 10). The foreign-born are 34.2 percent of all new business owners in California, which is consistent with previous findings on the importance of immigrants in California and the Silicon Valley (Saxenian, 1999, 2000, and Wadha et al., 2006). Roughly 5 percent of all new business owners in the United States are immigrants living in California. Immigrant-owned business creation is also substantial in other states; nearly 30 percent of all new business owners in New York, Florida, and Texas are immigrants—a substantially higher share than the national average of 16.7 percent. The top 10 states in terms of the number of new immigrant business owners are reported in the table. In the remaining states, immigrants represent only 6.3 percent of all new business owners, evidence of the geographical concentration of immigrants in the United States.

Table 8. Number of New Immigrant Business Owners per Month by Education Level Matched Current Population Survey (1996-2007)

Industry	New Immigrant Business Owners			All New Business Owners	
	Number	Percent of immigrant total	Percent of U.S. education total	Number	Percent of U.S. total
All education levels	81,100	100.0	16.7	484,864	100.0
Less than high school	28,001	34.5	35.8	78,195	16.1
High school graduate	20,686	25.5	13.8	149,824	30.9
Some college	13,281	16.4	10.4	127,928	26.4
College graduate	19,132	23.6	14.8	128,916	26.6

Notes: 1) The sample consists of individuals who do not own a business in the first survey month and report starting a business in the second survey month with 15 or more hours worked per week. 2) All reported estimates use sample weights provided by the CPS. Source: Author's calculations from matched 1996-2007 CPS microdata.

Table 9. Number of New Immigrant Business Owners per Month by Industry Matched Current Population Survey (1996-2007)

Industry	New immigrant business owners			All new business owners	
	Number	Percent of immigrant total	Percent of U.S. industry total	Number	Percent of U.S. total
All industries	80,659	100.0	16.7	483,743	100.0
Agriculture and mining	1,484	1.8	3.3	44,624	9.2
Construction	14,987	18.6	17.3	86,781	17.9
Manufacturing	2,367	2.9	15.1	15,664	3.2
Wholesale and retail trade	12,927	16.0	22.7	56,988	11.8
Transportation and utilities	4,254	5.3	23.1	18,439	3.8
Information	1,085	1.3	10.1	10,717	2.2
Financial activities	3,913	4.9	12.9	30,311	6.3
Professional and business services	14,864	18.4	15.7	94,484	19.5
Educational and health services	11,890	14.7	19.1	62,379	12.9
Leisure and hospitality	5,628	7.0	20.6	27,263	5.6
Other services	7,260	9.0	20.1	36,092	7.5

Notes: 1) The sample consists of individuals who do not own a business in the first survey month and report starting a business in the second survey month with 15 or more hours worked per week. 2) All reported estimates use sample weights provided by the CPS. Source: Author's calculations from matched 1996-2007 CPS microdata.

Immigrants contribute substantially to business starts in certain sectors and locations of the U.S. economy. The most notable contributions are geographic. In the four largest states immigrants constitute 30.6 percent of all new business owners. They are also roughly one-quarter of all new business owners in the transportation and utilities, and wholesale and retail trade industries.

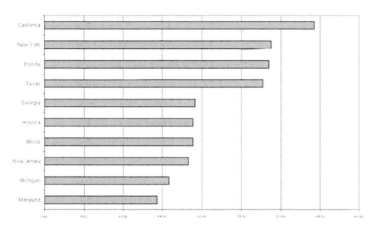

Figure 2. Immigrant Share of All New Business Owners for Top 10 States Matched Current Population Survey (1996-2007).

Table 10. Number of New Immigrant Business Owners per Month by State Matched Current Population Survey (1996-2007)

Industry	New immigrant business owners			All new business owners	
	Number	Percent of immigrant total	Percent of state total	Number	Percent of U.S. total
U.S. total	81,100	100.0	16.7	484,864	100.0
California	23,331	28.8	34.2	68,133	14.1
Texas	11,633	14.3	27.7	42,045	8.7
New York	8,953	11.0	28.7	31,169	6.4
Florida	8,026	9.9	28.4	28,214	5.8
Illinois	3,453	4.3	18.9	18,273	3.8
Georgia	3,023	3.7	19.1	15,786	3.3
Michigan	2,276	2.8	15.8	14,362	3.0
New Jersey	2,156	2.7	18.3	11,783	2.4
Arizona	2,000	2.5	18.9	10,584	2.2
Maryland	1,342	1.7	14.3	9,367	1.9
All other states	14,908	18.4	6.3	235,146	48.5

Notes: 1) The sample consists of individuals who do not own a business in the first survey month and report starting a business in the second survey month with 15 or more hours worked per week. 2) All reported estimates use sample weights provided by the CPS. 3) The reported states represent the largest 10 states based on the number of new businesses. Source: Author's calculations from matched 1996-2007 CPS microdata.

BUSINESS INCOME, SALES, AND EMPLOYMENT

The next question is how much immigrant-owned businesses contribute to total business income in the United States. How much value do they create for the U.S. economy? This is a difficult question to answer and measurement involves two approaches to the question. First, the 2000 Census includes information on business income net of all expenses reported by the individual business owner. The extremely large sample size of the Census is necessary to examine this question and to allow for examination of immigrant contributions by source country, education level, industry, and state. Second, the only large nationally representative *business-level* dataset that provides information on immigrant status, the 1992 Characteristics of Business Owners (CBO), is used to examine the sales and employment of immigrant-owned businesses.

Table 11 reports estimates from the 2000 Census on total business income for immigrant business owners. All estimates are reported in 2000 dollars. The total business income for immigrants is $67 billion, representing 11.6 percent of all business income in the United States. Total U.S. business income is $577 billion. The immigrant representation of total business income is lower than the representation of the total number of business owners, suggesting that immigrant-owned businesses have lower average incomes, an observation confirmed by estimates of average business income in Table 11. Immigrant-owned business income is $46,614 on average, compared with $50,643 for nonimmigrants.

Immigrant-owned businesses are also found to have lower levels of business income measured in logs. The log difference is around 3 percent. To check whether this business income disparity is because of differences in education and other demographic characteristics, the author estimates a log business income regression, which is reported in Specification 3 of Table 3. The estimates indicate that African American, Latino, and Native-American business owners each have substantially lower levels of business income than White business owners, and Asian-American business owners have slightly lower business income.[14] Similar to previous results, women business owners are found to have substantially lower business income than male owners (Gatewood et al., 2003, Lowrey, 2006, Fairlie and Robb, 2008). Business income generally increases with the age of the owner and is strongly related to the owner's education level. The general and specific knowledge and skills acquired through formal education may be useful for running a successful business. The owner's level of education may also serve as a proxy for overall ability or as a positive signal to potential customers, lenders, or other businesses.

Table 11. Total Business Income by Immigrant Group Census 2000.

Group	Net business income		
	Total (thousands of dollars)	Percent of U.S. total	Average per owner (dollars)
U.S. total	577,714,338	100.0	50,141
U.S.-born total	510,757,703	88.4	50,643
Immigrant total	66,956,635	11.6	46,614
Mexico	6,890,546	1.2	26,990
Korea	4,289,510	0.7	47,514
India	4,999,076	0.9	83,023
China	2,612,293	0.5	45,360
Vietnam	1,786,430	0.3	34,540
Canada	3,272,177	0.6	64,924
Cuba	2,421,547	0.4	49,334
Germany	2,322,318	0.4	56,054
Philippines	2,179,736	0.4	59,142
Italy	1,760,395	0.3	51,004
Iran	2,559,450	0.4	76,251
El Salvador	823,997	0.1	26,431
Poland	1,341,773	0.2	43,549
England	1,580,912	0.3	57,427
Colombia	883,144	0.2	34,284
Taiwan	1,367,917	0.2	58,266
Greece	1,253,056	0.2	60,441
Dominican Republic	536,080	0.1	26,860
Jamaica	672,985	0.1	35,448
Guatemala	422,663	0.1	22,588

Notes: 1) The sample consists of all workers with 15 or more hours worked per usual week. The total sample size is 596,550. 2) All reported estimates use sample weights provided by the 2000 Census. 3) Income estimates are reported in 2000 dollars. 4) The reported immigrant groups represent the largest 20 groups based on the number of business owners. Source: Author's calculations from 2000 Census microdata.

The immigrant coefficient is positive and statistically significant, but very small. The coefficient estimate implies that, after the findings are controlled for education and other demographic characteristics, immigrants are predicted to have business incomes roughly 2 percent higher than the U.S.-born. The difference is negligible and suggests that immigrant-owned businesses have similar business incomes when measured in logs.

Source Countries, Education, Industry, and State

Immigrants from Mexico provide the largest contribution to total U.S. business income at 1.2 percent. Korean and Indian immigrants make relatively large contributions to total business income, but overall the estimates reported in Table 10 indicate that immigrant contributions to total business income are spread across a very large number of immigrant groups in the United States, with no major groups dominating.

Unsurprisingly, most business income for both immigrants and the broader economy is produced by the most educated business owners. Table 12 reports estimates of immigrant business owner income by education level. Among immigrants, the total business income of college graduate business owners represents 52.1 percent of all immigrant-owned business income. Similarly, for all business owners, college graduates produce 51.9 percent of all business income. College-graduate immigrant business owners have $35 billion in business income. This sum represents 11.6 percent of all business income produced by college-educated business owners in the United States. Immigrant-owned businesses also generate a large share of total U.S. business income among the least educated.

Immigrant-owned businesses provide large income contributions to a few industries in the United States (see Table 13). In the arts, entertainment, and recreation industry they produce 21.1 percent of all business income. The next two largest industry contributions are in education, health, and social services (16.6 percent) and other services (16.1 percent).

Similar to their contributions to the numbers of business owners and starts, immigrants provide substantial contributions to total business income in the largest states. Table 14 reports estimates of the business income of immigrant business owners (Figure 3 displays the top 10 states). Immigrant business owners produce nearly $20 billion per year in California alone. This total represents nearly one-quarter of all business income produced in the state and

3.3 percent of all business income in the United States. In New York, Florida, and New Jersey, the total income of immigrant business owners represents nearly one-fifth of all business income. The income contributions of immigrant business owners to the economy are clearly unevenly spread across the country.

Sales and Employment

The 1992 Characteristics of Business Owners (CBO) contains information on the immigrant status of businesses in the United States. Two business outcomes are examined using these data— sales and employment. Published estimates from the CBO on the sales of immigrant-owned businesses are reported in Table 15 (U.S. Census Bureau, 1997). Several sales categories are reported because only categorical information is available in the published report.

Table 12. Total Net Business Income of Immigrant Business Owners by Education Level, Census 2000

Industry	Immigrant business owners			All business owners	
	Total business income (thousands of dollars)	Percent of immigrant total	Percent of U.S. education total	Total business income (dollars)	Percent of U.S. total
All education levels	66,956,635	100.0	11.6	577,714,338	100.0
Less than high school	10,283,783	15.4	25.8	39,936,703	6.9
High school graduate	9,642,336	14.4	9.5	101,236,676	17.5
Some college	12,148,724	18.1	8.9	136,799,688	23.7
College graduate	34,881,793	52.1	11.6	299,741,272	51.9

Notes: 1) The sample consists of all business owners with 15 or more hours worked per usual week. 2) All reported estimates use sample weights provided by the 2000 Census. Source: Author's calculations from 2000 Census microdata.

Table 13. Total Net Business Income of Immigrant Business Owners by Industry, Census 2000

Industry	Immigrant business owners			All business owners	
	Total business income (thousands of dollars)	Percent of immigrant total	Percent of U.S. industry total	Total business income (dollars)	Percent of U.S. total
All Industries	66,956,635	100.0	11.6	577,714,339	100.0
Agriculture and mining	863,382	1.3	3.6	23,733,994	4.1
Construction	7,270,433	10.9	8.9	81,803,394	14.2
Manufacturing	3,826,155	5.7	13.1	29,227,633	5.1
Wholesale trade	3,496,142	5.2	14.6	24,020,513	4.2
Retail trade	7,061,513	10.5	14.6	48,498,327	8.4
Transportation	2,646,458	4.0	14.0	18,956,561	3.3
Information	846,904	1.3	9.6	8,864,787	1.5
Finance, insurance and real estate	5,138,095	7.7	8.1	63,586,517	11.0
Professional services	11,018,063	16.5	8.1	135,541,200	23.5
Education, health, and social services	14,327,217	21.4	16.6	86,492,345	15.0
Arts, entertainment, and recreation	5,448,776	8.1	21.1	25,825,562	4.5
Other services	5,013,499	7.5	16.1	31,163,505	5.4

Notes: 1) The sample consists of all business owners with 15 or more hours worked per usual week. 2) All reported estimates use sample weights provided by the 2000 Census. 3) Income estimates are reported in 2000 dollars. Source: Author's calculations from 2000 Census microdata.

Table 14. Total Net Business Income of Immigrant Business Owners by State Census 2000

Industry	Immigrant business owners			All business owners	
	Total business income (thousands of dollars)	Percent of immigrant total	Percent of state total	Total business income (dollars)	Percent of U.S. total
U.S. total	66,956,635	100.0	11.6	577,714,338	100.0
Alabama	256,104	0.4	3.6	7,166,173	1.2
Alaska	69,040	0.1	5.7	1,212,297	0.2
Arizona	964,106	1.4	10.0	9,644,560	1.7
Arkansas	84,821	0.1	1.7	4,871,000	0.8
California	19,238,566	28.7	22.7	84,779,273	14.7
Colorado	732,304	1.1	6.1	12,001,064	2.1
Connecticut	1,109,478	1.7	10.9	10,138,100	1.8
Delaware	94,554	0.1	6.6	1,429,332	0.2
District of Columbia	174,008	0.3	12.4	1,400,518	0.2
Florida	6,649,952	9.9	18.7	35,561,024	6.2
Georgia	1,275,188	1.9	7.5	16,971,110	2.9
Hawaii	416,814	0.6	17.4	2,392,770	0.4
Idaho	89,535	0.1	3.2	2,774,498	0.5
Illinois	3,391,939	5.1	13.3	25,554,039	4.4
Indiana	463,032	0.7	4.5	10,317,542	1.8
Iowa	151,152	0.2	2.7	5,541,212	1.0
Kansas	168,809	0.3	3.1	5,476,371	0.9
Kentucky	175,571	0.3	2.7	6,385,840	1.1
Louisiana	342,347	0.5	4.6	7,430,561	1.3
Maine	106,948	0.2	3.8	2,847,483	0.5
Maryland	1,474,148	2.2	13.0	11,304,225	2.0
Massachusetts	1,571,727	2.3	10.6	14,892,847	2.6
Michigan	1,475,603	2.2	8.4	17,650,532	3.1
Minnesota	330,847	0.5	3.0	10,944,980	1.9
Mississippi	134,162	0.2	2.9	4,562,312	0.8

Table 14. (Continued)

Industry	Immigrant business owners			All business owners	
	Total business income (thousands of dollars)	Percent of immigrant total	Percent of state total	Total business income (dollars)	Percent of U.S. total
Missouri	395,880	0.6	4.0	9,897,877	1.7
Montana	50,158	0.1	2.5	2,046,671	0.4
Nebraska	52,780	0.1	1.5	3,520,465	0.6
Nevada	340,279	0.5	9.3	3,650,124	0.6
New Hampshire	170,711	0.3	5.8	2,928,503	0.5
New Jersey	3,793,618	5.7	18.0	21,125,412	3.7
New Mexico	218,281	0.3	7.1	3,077,300	0.5
New York	7,872,297	11.8	19.2	40,998,879	7.1
North Carolina	707,484	1.1	4.7	15,201,153	2.6
North Dakota	23,721	0.0	1.7	1,376,842	0.2
Ohio	1,050,359	1.6	5.5	18,989,629	3.3
Oklahoma	213,901	0.3	3.6	5,887,341	1.0
Oregon	549,137	0.8	6.9	7,930,674	1.4
Pennsylvania	1,391,227	2.1	6.6	21,092,206	3.7
Rhode Island	186,956	0.3	9.5	1,963,461	0.3
South Carolina	267,477	0.4	4.0	6,739,441	1.2
South Dakota	45,763	0.1	2.5	1,850,081	0.3
Tennessee	411,043	0.6	3.8	10,732,160	1.9
Texas	4,952,249	7.4	12.2	40,678,349	7.0
Utah	174,255	0.3	4.1	4,223,437	0.7
Vermont	84,016	0.1	5.4	1,554,292	0.3
Virginia	1,380,549	2.1	10.2	13,524,141	2.3
Washington	1,253,575	1.9	9.8	12,812,259	2.2
West Virginia	167,461	0.3	7.9	2,118,930	0.4
Wisconsin	246,080	0.4	2.6	9,505,478	1.6
Wyoming	16,625	0.0	1.6	1,039,570	0.2

Notes: 1) The sample includes all business owners with 15 or more hours worked per usual week. 2) All reported estimates use sample weights provided by the 2000 Census. 3) Income estimates are reported in 2000 dollars. Source: Author's calculations from 2000 Census microdata.

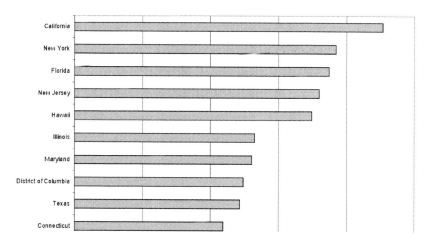

Figure 3. Immigrant Share of Total Business Income for Top 10 States Census 2000.

Immigrant-owned businesses represent 9.4 percent of all businesses in the United States. This estimate is lower than the 12.5 percent reported for business owners partly because the data are from 1992 before the large number of immigrants arrived in the 1990s. The CBO also contains a large number of small-scale businesses and consulting activities, whereas the Census and CPS data contain only workers whose primary job activity is business ownership (see the discussion in Section 3 above). The estimate of the total number of businesses from the CBO is 17.3 million, which is considerably larger than the 11.5 million estimate of the number of business owners from the Census Bureau.

Direct evidence of the inclusion of small-scale business and consulting activities is provided by the large share (30.3 percent) of firms with less than $5,000 in revenues.[15] Immigrant-owned businesses constitute only 6.8 percent of all businesses in the less than $5,000 sales category. If this category is removed, immigrants represent 10.1 percent of all businesses.

Immigrants own a significant share of high sales firms—10.8 percent of all firms with $100,000 or more and 9.2 percent of all firms with $1 million or more in sales.

Table 15. Number of Immigrant-Owned Businesses by Sales Level Characteristics of Business Owners (1992)

Sales level	Immigrant-owned firms			All firms	
	Number	Percent of immigrant total	Percent of U.S. sales level total	Number	Percent of U.S. total
All businesses	1,617,482	100.0	9.4	17,253,143	100.0
Less than $5,000	355,586	22.0	6.8	5,226,553	30.3
$5,000-$9,999	221,440	13.7	9.1	2,443,946	14.2
$10,000-$24,999	285,574	17.7	9.3	3,076,410	17.8
$25,000-$49,999	202,430	12.5	10.4	1,945,806	11.3
$50,000-$99,999	192,743	11.9	11.9	1,615,940	9.4
$100,000-$199,999	134,114	8.3	11.2	1,197,996	6.9
$200,000-$249,999	26,581	1.6	8.8	301,794	1.7
$250,000-$499,999	86,260	5.3	12.6	682,583	4.0
$500,000-$999,999	35,611	2.2	9.6	372,078	2.2
$1,000,000 or more	35,851	2.2	9.2	390,037	2.3
$100,000 or more	318,417	19.7	10.8	2,944,488	17.1

Note: The sample consists of businesses that are classified by the IRS as individual proprietorships or self-employed persons, partnerships, and subchapter S corporations and that have sales of $500 or more.

Source: Auhor's calculations based on published estimates from the 1992 CBO (U.S. Census Bureau 1997).

The CBO also provides estimates of employment for several employment levels. Table 16 reports estimates of the number of immigrant-owned businesses for several employment categories. Immigrant-owned firms constitute 8.9 percent of all firms with no employees. In comparison, immigrants own 10.8 percent of all firms with employees. Ownership shares of the largest employment classes are lower among immigrants, however. Immigrants own 6.8 percent of all firms with 50-99 employees and 5.5 percent of all firms with 100 or more employees.

Table 16. Number of Immigrant-Owned Businesses by Employment Size Characteristics of Business Owners (1992)

Revenues	Immigrant-owned firms			All firms	
	Number	Percent of immigrant total	Percent of U.S. employment size total	Number	Percent of U.S. total
All businesses	1,617,482	100.0	9.4	17,253,143	100.0
No paid employees	1,258,657	77.8	8.9	14,118,184	81.8
With paid employees	339,995	21.0	10.8	3,134,959	18.2
Less than 5 employees	243,335	15.0	11.3	2,151,914	12.5
5 to 9 employees	53,325	3.3	10.6	503,808	2.9
10 to 19 employees	25,388	1.6	9.9	256,110	1.5
20 to 49 employees	13,042	0.8	9.0	144,734	0.8
50 to 99 employees	3,100	0.2	6.8	45,331	0.3
100 or more employees	1,805	0.1	5.5	33,062	0.2

Note: The sample includes businesses that are classified by the IRS as individual proprietorships or self-employed persons, partnerships, and subchapter S corporations and that have sales of $500 or more.

Source: Auhor's calculations based on published estimates from the 1992 CBO (U.S. Census Bureau 1997).

CONCLUSIONS

Immigrant business owners make important contributions to the U.S. economy. They start 16.7 percent of all new businesses in the United States and represent 12.5 percent of all business owners. The large contribution of immigrants to the number of business owners and new business owners in the United States is partly fueled by relatively high rates of business ownership and formation among immigrants. For example, immigrants are 30 percent more likely to start businesses each month than are nonimmigrants. Immigrant business owners also contribute substantially to total U.S. business income, sales, and employment. Of total business income in the United States, 11.6 percent is generated by immigrant business owners. Immigrant-owned businesses constitute 11.2 percent of all U.S. businesses with $100,000 or more in annual sales and 10.8 percent of all firms with employees. Although in total counts and dollars, immigrants from Mexico contribute the most to total U.S. business ownership, formation, and income, immigrants from around the world make important contributions.

Immigrants are found to contribute even more to specific sectors of the U.S. economy. Immigrant-owned businesses constitute a large share of business ownership, starts and income in the lowest- and highest-skilled businesses, and in the arts, entertainment and recreation, other services, wholesale and retail trade, and transportation industries. Immigrant-owned businesses provide very large business contributions to several states in the country. Immigrants represent 30 percent of all business owners in California, one-fourth in New York, and more than one-fifth in New Jersey, Florida, and Hawaii. Slightly more than one-third of all new business owners in California and nearly 30 percent in New York, Florida, and Texas are immigrants. Finally, immigrant business owners generate nearly one-quarter of all business income in California, and 3.3 percent of all business income in the United States. In New York, Florida, and New Jersey, total immigrant-owned business income represents nearly one-fifth of all business income.

The findings from this analysis contribute to the understanding of immigrant business ownership and the contributions of immigrant business owners to the U.S. economy and have implications for the ongoing debates about immigration policy. The evidence presented here indicates that immigrants make significant contributions to business ownership, formation, and income in the United States. The economic contributions of immigrant business owners are also unevenly distributed across the United States, with the largest contributions located in California and other "gateway" states.

REFERENCES

Advanced Research Technologies, LLC. (2005). *The innovation-entrepreneurship NEXUS: A national assessment of entrepreneurship and regional economic growth and development*. Washington, D.C.: U.S. Small Business Administration, Office of Advocacy.

Bjelland, M., Haltiwanger, J., Sandusky, K. & Spletzer, J. (2006). *Reconciling household and administrative measures of self-employment and entrepreneurship.* Washington, D.C.: U.S. Census Bureau working paper.

Borjas, G. (1986). The self-employment experience of immigrants. *Journal of Human Resources, 21*, Fall: 487-506.

Burton, John A. (2005). *Putting the spotlight on small business*, Center for American Progress.

Davis, S. J., Haltiwanger, J., Jarmin, R., Krizan, C. J., Miranda, J., Nucci, A. & Sandusky, K. (2006). *Measuring the dynamics of young and small businesses: Integrating the employer and nonemployer universes.* (CES working paper no. 06-04, February.)

Fairlie, R. W. (2008). *The Kauffman index of entrepreneurial activity: 1996-2007.* Kansas City, MO: The Ewing Marion Kauffman Foundation.

Fairlie, R. W. (2007). *Entrepreneurship in Silicon Valley during the boom and bust*, Washington, DC: U.S. Small Business Administration, Office of Advocacy, Washington, D.C.

Fairlie, R. & Robb, A. (2008) *Race and entrepreneurial success: Black-, Asian-, and White-owned businesses in the United States.* Cambridge, MA: MIT Press.

Fairlie R. W., Zissimopoulos, J. & Krashinsky, H. A. (2008). The international Asian business success story: A comparison of Chinese, Indian, and other Asian businesses in the United States, Canada, and United Kingdom. *International differences in entrepreneurship*, in J.Lerner and A. Shoar, eds. Washington, D.C.: National Bureau of Economic Research Press (forthcoming).

Gatewood, E. G., Carter, N. M., Brush, C. G., Greene, P. G. & Hart, M. M. (2003). *Women entrepreneurs, their ventures, and the venture capital industry: An annotated bibliography.* Stockholm: ESBRI.

Headd, B. (2005). *Business estimates from the Office of Advocacy: A discussion of methodology.* Washington, D.C.: U.S. Small Business Administration, Office of Advocacy working paper.

Headd, B. & Saade, R. (2008). *Do business definition decisions distort small business results?* Washington, D.C. : U.S. Small Business Administration, Office of Advocacy working paper.

Lowrey, Y. (2006). *Women in business, 2006. A demographic review of women's business ownership.* Washington, D.C.: U.S. Small Business Administration, Office of Advocacy.

Lowrey, Y. (2007). *Minorities in business: A demographic review of minority business ownership.* Washington, D.C.: U.S. Small Business Administration, Office of Advocacy.

Moutray, C. (2007). *Educational attainment and other characteristics of the self-employed: An examination using the Panel Study of Income Dynamics data.* Washington, D.C.: U.S. Small Business Administration, Office of Advocacy working paper.

Parker, S. C. (2004). *The economics of self-employment and entrepreneurship.* Cambridge: Cambridge University Press.

Reynolds, P. D., Bygrave, W. D. & Autio, E. (2003). *Global Entrepreneurship Monitor: 2003 executive report.* Babson College, London Business School and the Kauffman Foundation.

Saxenian, A. (1999). *Silicon Valley's new immigrant entrepreneurs,* San Francisco: Public Policy Institute of California.

Saxenian, A. (2000). Networks of immigrant entrepreneurs. In *The Silicon Valley edge: A habitat for innovation and entrepreneurship.* C. Lee, W. F. Miller, and H. S. Rowen, eds. Stanford: Stanford University Press.

Schuetze, H. J. & Antecol, H. (2007). Immigration, entrepreneurship and the venture start-up process. *The life cycle of entrepreneurial ventures: International handbook series on entrepreneurship, vol. 3,* S. Parker, ed. Springer: New York.

U.S. Census Bureau. (1997). *1992 Economic Census: Characteristics of Business Owners.* Washington, D.C.: U.S. Government Printing Office.

U.S. Census Bureau. (2006). *2002 Economic Census, Survey of Business Owners,* Washington, D.C.: U.S. Government Printing Office.

U.S. Census Bureau. (2006). 2002 *Economic Census, Survey of Business Owners, Characteristics of Business Owners*, Washington, D.C.: U.S. Government Printing Office.

U.S. Department of Homeland Security. (2007). *2007 yearbook of immigration statistics,* Washington, D.C.: Office of Immigration Statistics, http://www.dhs.gov/ximgtn/statistics/publications/yearbook.shtm.

U.S. Small Business Administration, Office of Advocacy. (2001). *Private firms, establishments, employment, annual payroll and receipts by firm size, 1998-2001.* Table reported at http://www.sba.gov/advo/stats/us_tot.pdf.

van der Sluis, J., van Praag, M. & Vijverberg, W. (2004). *Education and entrepreneurship in industrialized countries: A meta-analysis.* Tinbergen Institute working paper no. TI 03–046/3. Amsterdam: Tinbergen Institute.

Wadhwa, V., Saxenian, A., Ris sing, B. & Gereff, G. (2007). *America's new immigrant entrepreneurs.* Durham, NC: Duke University.

End Notes

[1] Although the cross-sectional CPS data are commonly used to estimate static rates of business ownership, the matched data allow for the creation of a dynamic measure of entrepreneurship that captures the rate of business formation at the individual owner level.

[2] National estimates for several demographic groups and state-level estimates created from these microdata are reported in the Kauffman Index of Entrepreneurial Activity (Fairlie, 2008).

[3] Some unemployed individuals may report being self-employed if they sell a small quantity of goods or services while not working at their regular jobs.

[4] Regularly published estimates from the CPS by the U.S. Bureau of Labor Statistics, such as those reported in *Employment and Earnings*, however, exclude incorporated business owners, who represent roughly one- third of all business owners.

[5] The Total Entrepreneurial Activity (TEA) index used in the Global Entrepreneurship Monitor captures individuals who are involved in either the startup phase or managing a business that is less than 42 months old (Reynolds, Bygrave, and Autio, 2003).

[6] These data are now available for downloading from http://www.kauffman.org/kauffmanindex/.

[7] See Fairlie and Robb (2008) for more discussion of the availability of owner information in business-level datasets.

[8] These estimates differ from published estimates reported in U.S. Census Bureau (2006) because they exclude publicly held, foreign-owned, not-for-profit, and other firms (Fairlie and Robb, 2008).

[9] One difference is that the 1992 CBO excludes C corporations, whereas the 2002 SBO includes them.

[10] Estimates from the SUSB are reported by the U.S. Small Business Administration, Office of Advocacy (see www.sba.gov/advo/research/data.html). See also the Advanced Research Technologies, LLC (2005) report to the U.S. Small Business Administration, and Burton: Center for American Progress (2005) for results for detailed geographical areas.

[11] Marginal effects are estimated using the coefficient estimates and the full sample distribution. They provide an estimate of the effect of a 1 unit change in the explanatory variable on the probability of business ownership.

[12] Conditional on two groups having similar business ownership rates, the only way that one group can have a higher business entry rate is if it also has a higher business exit rate (see Fairlie, 2006, and Fairlie and Robb, 2008, for more discussion).

[13] Estimates of immigrant-owned business starts are reported only for the 10 largest immigrant groups because sample sizes are not large enough. Although the number of non-business owners is large for each source country, the number of new business owners per month recorded in the data is relatively small (0.28 percent).

[14] See Lowrey (2007) and Fairlie and Robb (2008) for recent evidence on racial patterns in business performance.

[15] The CBO sample consists of individuals who file an IRS form 1040 Schedule C (individual proprietorship or self-employed person), 1065 (partenership), or 1120S (subchanpter S corporation), and have at least 500 or more in revenues.

INDEX

A

accounting, 2, 19, 34, 38, 43
achievement, 11
adaptation, 66
adjustment, 7, 40
administration, 66
administrative, 105
adult, 74
adults, 17, 73
age, 2, 14, 21, 22, 25, 27, 29, 30, 73, 74, 79, 82, 88, 94
agricultural, 4
agricultural economics, 4
agriculture, 77
alertness, 11, 12
alternative, 49, 66
AMS, 44
argument, 9
assessment, 45, 50, 104
attacker, 45
attitudes, 13
availability, 40, 107

B

barriers, 13, 45
bed, 4, 6
behavior, 13
beliefs, 14
benefits, 4, 5, 6, 14, 40
Best Practice, 48
bias, 16
biotechnology, 48
birth, 16, 19, 76, 77
blocks, 14
bonding, 14
brain drain, 50
Bureau of the Census, 74
business model, 2, 42
bust, 105

C

calculus, 13
capital accumulation, 2
capitalism, 44, 46, 49
Census, viii, 12, 29, 31, 36, 69, 72, 73, 74, 75, 76, 77, 78, 79, 80, 81, 82, 83, 84, 85, 86, 87, 89, 94, 95, 97, 98, 99, 100, 101, 102, 103, 105, 106, 107
Census Bureau, 12, 31, 75, 76, 77, 78, 97, 101, 102, 103, 105, 106, 107
CEO, 16, 17
CES, 105
chemicals, 50, 51
children, 11, 81, 82
citizens, 2, 3, 7, 16, 33, 43, 47, 66
citizenship, 20, 40
classes, 102
classical, 4
clusters, 42

coal, 51
codes, 66, 74
communities, 15, 16, 42
comparative research, 42
competence, 41
competition, 4, 5, 10, 49
competitive advantage, 7
competitiveness, 48
complementarity, 42
components, 51
Comprehensive Immigration Reform Act, 47
computer science, 12
concentrates, 16, 20, 66
concentration, 91
conditioning, 73
confidence, 4, 11
consensus, 46
constraints, 41
consulting, 101
continuity, 66
contractors, 9
control, 21, 25, 43, 79
corn, 46
corporations, 76, 102, 103, 107
costs, 14, 46
country-of-origin, 73
covering, 5
CPS, 70, 72, 73, 74, 75, 76, 77, 78, 81, 88, 90, 91, 92, 93, 101, 107
creative thinking, 43
cross-border, 29
cross-sectional, 73, 107
Current Population Survey (CPS), viii, 69, 72, 74
customers, 3, 56, 95

D

data availability, 71
data processing, 19, 52
database, 17, 29, 34
death, 19
decisions, 14, 105
definition, 19, 50, 66, 67, 73, 105

democracy, 48, 49
demographic characteristics, 75, 79, 88, 89, 94, 96
demographics, 22
Department of Defense, 4
Department of Homeland Security, 7, 71, 76, 78, 84, 106
Department of State, 41
dependent variable, 21, 28, 79, 81, 88
developed countries, 71
diaspora, 47
discrimination, 14
disposition, 20
distillation, 11
distribution, 8, 51, 82, 83, 107
diversity, 13, 48
division, 55
dominance, 14
doors, 47
duration, 33

E

earnings, 9
echoing, 9
ecology, 5
economic activity, viii, 1
economic adaptation, 49
economic development, 3, 4, 6, 41, 45, 48
economic growth, vii, 1, 4, 5, 9, 18, 43, 46, 50, 88, 104
economic performance, 25, 28
economic policy, 46
economics, 44, 48, 106
education, 10, 32, 34, 47, 83, 84, 85, 89, 91, 96, 97, 98, 106
educational attainment, 12
educational background, 20
educational system, 8
elders, 5
elephants, 44
emigration, 10
employees, 5, 17, 25, 27, 70, 102, 103, 104
employers, 7, 10, 40, 49

employment, 7, 8, 10, 11, 14, 15, 19, 21, 25, 27, 29, 30, 40, 41, 44, 45, 46, 47, 50, 66, 70, 71, 72, 77, 94, 97, 102, 103, 104, 105, 106
employment growth, 19, 66
entertainment, 84, 85, 96, 104
entrepreneurs, vii, viii, 1, 2, 3, 11, 12, 13, 14, 15, 16, 17, 29, 33, 40, 41, 42, 43, 48, 49, 50, 66, 69, 71, 105, 106, 107
entrepreneurship, vii, 1, 2, 3, 4, 5, 6, 7, 11, 12, 13, 14, 15, 16, 39, 41, 42, 43, 44, 45, 46, 47, 48, 49, 71, 74, 75, 104, 105, 106, 107
environment, 5
estimating, 75, 79
ethnic groups, 16
ethnicity, 14, 38, 47, 57, 59, 61, 63, 65
evolution, 45
exclusion, 78
expertise, 3
exploitation, 11, 13, 14
exposure, 13
externalities, 5

F

failure, 10, 14
false positive, 74
family, 7, 8, 29, 41, 82
family members, 7
family relationships, 29
federal government, 6, 41
feedback, 13
females, 37
finance, 3, 9
financial support, 14
firm size, 106
firms, 4, 5, 6, 17, 18, 21, 33, 44, 45, 46, 50, 56, 71, 73, 76, 77, 78, 101, 102, 103, 104, 106, 107
flight, 46
flow, 4, 8, 10, 13, 78, 88
focusing, 66
folklore, 14
foreign firms, 56

foreign-born population, 21, 22
formal education, 3, 94
funding, 6
funds, 6

G

gas, 50
gender, 14, 20, 36, 38, 82
General Electric, 4
generalization, 38
glass, 16
global leaders, 7
goods and services, 11, 73
government, iv, viii, 2, 6, 15, 41, 43, 53, 54, 69, 74, 76
graduate students, 9, 12, 29
groups, 16, 22, 27, 42, 71, 72, 79, 80, 83, 89, 90, 95, 96, 107
growth, vii, 1, 2, 3, 4, 5, 6, 9, 12, 15, 18, 19, 42, 43, 44, 46, 49, 50, 53, 66, 88, 104
guidance, 15

H

habitat, 106
health, 85, 92, 96, 98
health services, 92
high school, 8, 33, 57, 59, 60, 62, 64, 83, 84, 88, 90, 91, 97
high school degree, 33, 83
high tech, 46
higher education, 3, 12, 40
high-tech, vii, 1, 2, 3, 5, 6, 7, 9, 10, 11, 12, 13, 14, 15, 16, 18, 19, 33, 36, 37, 39, 40, 41, 42, 43, 44, 45, 49, 50, 66, 71
hip, 7
homeland security, 7, 71, 76, 78, 84, 106
hospital, 52
hospitality, 90, 92
house, 9
household, 69, 74, 77, 105
hub, 10
hypothesis, 42

I

IBM, 4
IFN, 46
illusions, 49
immigrants, vii, viii, 1, 3, 8, 9, 10, 12, 13, 14, 16, 42, 45, 66, 69, 70, 71, 72, 75, 78, 79, 82, 83, 84, 88, 89, 91, 92, 94, 96, 101, 102, 103, 104, 105
immigration, 3, 4, 7, 8, 9, 10, 14, 40, 41, 42, 45, 47, 48, 50, 66, 67, 104, 106
Immigration and Customs Enforcement, 49
incentives, 48, 66
inclusion, 101
income, vii, viii, 10, 69, 70, 72, 73, 75, 78, 81, 94, 95, 96, 97, 98, 99, 100, 103, 104
independent variable, 81
indication, 70
indicators, 28
individual characteristics, 82
industrial, 4, 5, 46, 51, 54, 73
industrial policy, 46
industrialized countries, 106
industry, 9, 19, 29, 48, 50, 51, 54, 84, 85, 90, 92, 94, 96, 98, 105
Information Technology, 46
inheritance, 47
innovation, 3, 4, 6, 7, 45, 47, 48, 49, 50, 88, 104, 106
inorganic, 50
instruments, 51
insurance, 85
intellectual property, 6
international migration, 47, 66
interview, 48, 73
inventions, 47
inventors, 9
investment, 6, 40, 66
investors, 49

J

job creation, vii, 1, 3, 5, 15, 18, 43
job skills, 8

jobs, 5, 8, 12, 17, 18, 45, 71, 88

L

labor, 3, 9, 12, 13, 45, 48
labor force, 3, 12
land, 3, 11
language, 12, 13, 40
language barrier, 13
language skills, 13
large-scale, 4
law, 9, 40
legal permanent residents, 76, 78
legislation, 66
leisure, 90
lenders, 95
lenses, 51
life cycle, 106
life experiences, 42
lifetime, 40
likelihood, 38
linear, 21, 81
linear regression, 21, 81
linkage, 7
links, 19
longevity, 79
lower-income, 10
lying, 27

M

machinery, 51
machines, 51
management, 13, 50, 67
manufacturing, 19, 21, 22
marital status, 79, 81, 82
market, 3, 9, 13, 45
markets, 12
marriage, 7, 38
mathematics, 8, 29
measurement, 77, 94
measures, 9, 27, 69, 74, 75, 105
melting, 7
membership, 15, 34

men, 82
meta-analysis, 106
metropolitan area, 41
mice, 44
migrants, 10
migration, 10, 42, 47, 48, 66
mining, 85, 92, 98
minorities, 37, 38, 42
minority, 37, 38, 106
missiles, 51
MIT, 16, 44, 46, 49, 105
mobility, 49
models, 2, 42, 79
momentum, 7
money, 14
movement, 10
multinational companies, 4, 5
multivariate, 27, 28, 79

N

nation, 2, 40, 43
National Academy of Sciences, 9, 48
National Aeronautics and Space Administration, 4
national culture, 8
National Institute of Standards and Technology, 6
nationality, 7
Native American, 81, 82, 88
Native Hawaiian, 39, 57, 59, 61, 63, 65
natural, 41, 50
natural gas, 50
non-citizen, 47
nonimmigrants, 70, 72, 82, 88, 94, 103
non-profit, 52
non-random, 21
normal distribution, 82
not-for-profit, 107

O

observations, 73, 74
occupational, 12, 47

occupational background, 12
offshore, 9
oligopoly, 4
on-line, 48
optimism, 14
organic, 6, 51, 66
organic chemicals, 51
organic growth, 6, 66
outsourcing, 9
ownership, vii, viii, 19, 69, 70, 71, 72, 73, 74, 75, 77, 78, 79, 80, 81, 82, 83, 85, 87, 88, 101, 103, 104, 105, 106, 107

P

partnerships, 77, 102, 103
patents, 20, 27, 43, 55
payroll, 106
pension, 6
permanent resident, 7
permit, 7
petroleum, 50, 51
pharmaceuticals, 54
phone, 53
plants, 5, 6, 66
play, viii, 1, 3, 15, 41, 43, 67
policy initiative, 6
policy makers, , 5, 7, 8, 49
population, 10, 12, 15, 18, 19, 20, 21, 29, 33, 42, 74, 75, 83
portfolios, 6
positive externalities, 18
private sector, 19
probability, 14, 21, 79, 81, 88, 107
probe, 54
problem solving, 44
production function, 49
productivity growth, 2, 5
profit, 52, 107
program, 6, 7, 9, 10, 20, 45, 50, 71
prosperity, 2, 44
proxy, 83, 94
public policy, 4, 44, 46
public relations, 50, 67
P-value, 21, 30

Q

qualifications, 40
quality assurance, 20
questionnaire, 20

R

race, 20, 36, 57, 59, 61, 63, 65, 67, 74
random, 18
range, 22, 78
real estate, 77, 85, 98
recognition, 11, 13
recreation, 84, 85, 96, 98, 104
recruiting, 9
refining, 51
reforms, 47
refugees, 76, 78
regression, 21, 25, 27, 28, 30, 79, 81, 89, 94
regression method, 21
regular jobs, 107
relationship, 2, 20, 21, 28, 29, 42, 43, 56, 82
relaxation, 6
research and development, 55
resistance, 8
resources, 2, 3, 14, 20, 44
retail, 84, 90, 92, 104
returns, 46
revenue, 25
risk, 2, 13, 14
risk-taking, 13
rolling, 51
rubber, 51

S

salaries, 10, 56
salary, 75, 77, 82
sales, 16, 17, 19, 66, 70, 71, 72, 77, 94, 97, 101, 102, 103, 104
sample, vii, 1, 2, 3, 18, 21, 22, 27, 29, 33, 36, 37, 38, 39, 40, 42, 43, 72, 73, 74, 80, 81, 84, 85, 87, 88, 90, 91, 92, 93, 94, 95, 97, 98, 100, 102, 103, 107
sampling, 18
satisfaction, 13
SBA, 19, 44, 78
school, 8, 29, 31, 33, 40, 52, 57, 59, 60, 61, 62, 64, 65, 81, 83, 84, 88, 90, 91, 97
search, 12
seedlings, 5
self-employed, 73, 74, 76, 77, 102, 103, 106, 107
self-employment, 15, 44, 45, 77, 105, 106
sex, 74
shaping, 4, 41
shares, 22, 72, 83, 102
SIC, 19, 26, 27, 30, 50, 52, 66, 67
signals, 9
silicon, 5, 10, 16, 17, 42, 47, 71, 91, 105, 106
skills, 3, 8, 13, 47, 94
Small Business Administration, 1, 15, 45, 49, 53, 54, 69, 78, 104, 105, 106, 107
small firms, 44
small-scale business, 73, 77, 101
smokestacks, 6
social capital, 14, 29
social context, 8, 46
social institutions, 14
social services, 85, 96, 98
socialism, 49
software, 54
specific knowledge, 94
spectrum, 33
spin, 12
sponsor, 40
standard error, 81
statistics, 106
stereotype, 14
stereotypical, 14
stock, 78, 87, 88
strategies, 10, 42, 50
strength, 21
students, 7, 8, 9, 12, 29, 40, 44, 47
substitutes, 9, 41
supervisors, 20

suppliers, 3, 56
supply, 11, 12, 47
supply chain, 12

T

talent, 3, 7, 10, 14, 41, 44, 46, 47
taste, 8
technological change, 49
technology transfer, 6
telephone, 20
textile, 50
threshold, 16
timing, 11
title, 54
total employment, 19, 50
total revenue, 19, 50
trade, 84, 85, 90, 92, 98, 104
traffic, 66
training, 12, 20, 40, 49
trajectory, 13
transfer, 6, 53
transnationalism, 15, 66
transportation, 51, 84, 90, 92, 104
trust, 14

U

U.S. Citizenship and Immigration Services, 7
U.S. economy, vii, viii, 1, 15, 19, 45, 69, 71, 72, 83, 84, 88, 89, 92, 94, 103, 104
Ukraine, 35
uncertainty, 41
undergraduate, 2, 9, 43
unemployment, 73
universe, 18

universities, 7, 12, 46
urbanicity, 81

V

values, 12, 21, 28, 79
variables, 18, 21, 25, 27, 28, 30, 43, 81, 82
variation, 38, 67
vehicles, 6, 51
venture capital, 5, 6, 14, 15, 16, 46, 105
visa, 7, 9, 10, 40, 47, 66, 71
visible, 12, 16

W

wages, 8, 9, 48, 56
weakness, 18
wealth, 8, 71
weathering, 2
welfare, 44
wholesale, 84, 90, 92, 104
wireless, 20
wisdom, 5
women, 37, 42, 94, 105
work activity, 77
workers, 8, 9, 10, 12, 40, 44, 47, 49, 71, 74, 76, 77, 80, 81, 95, 101
workforce, 6, 29, 30, 47, 48
World Bank, 47
World War, 4, 5

Y

yield, 18